Confessions of a Former Child

*It takes a long time
to become young.*
—**Pablo Picasso**

Confessions of a Former Child

A Therapist's Memoir

Daniel J. Tomasulo

Graywolf Press
SAINT PAUL, MINNESOTA

Publication of this volume is made possible in part by a grant provided by the Minnesota State Arts Board, through an appropriation by the Minnesota State Legislature; a grant from the Wells Fargo Foundation Minnesota; and a grant from the National Endowment for the Arts, which believes that a great nation deserves great art. Significant support has also been provided by the Bush Foundation; Target; the McKnight Foundation; and other generous contributions from foundations, corporations, and individuals. To these organizations and individuals we offer our heartfelt thanks.

Published by Graywolf Press
2402 University Avenue, Suite 203
Saint Paul, Minnesota 55114
All rights reserved

www.graywolfpress.org

Published in the United States of America

ISBN 978-1-55597-499-2

2 4 6 8 9 7 5 3 1
First Graywolf Printing, 2008

Library of Congress Control Number: 2007940216

Cover design: www.VetoDesignUSA.com
Cover photo: iStockphoto
Interior photos: Author's collection

. . . students of history continue to ignore the simple facts that all individuals are borne by mothers; that everybody was once a child; . . . and that society consists of individuals in the process of developing from children into parents.
—Erik Erikson

. . . your parents were the first instruments God used to bring you into the world, and so must they be the instruments through which you shall return.
—Lawrence Kushner

For my parents Marge and Artie,
my sister Donna,
my wife Nancy,
and my daughter Devon.

Author's Note

Out of respect for their privacy I have changed the names of some of the people who appear in this book. When referring to individuals I have worked with in therapy, I have followed the American Psychological Association's guideline to protect confidentiality.

Contents

Prologue

We can easily forgive a child who is afraid of the dark;
the real tragedy of life is when men are afraid of the light.
—**Plato**

As a child I always found delight in my daydreams. It was the night that gave me trouble. A recurring dream throughout childhood left me exhausted and disheartened. Not a nightmare really, but an endless, impossible effort to solve a puzzle. Literally.

In my dream a brilliant light radiated from the center of an unsolved jigsaw puzzle. I had the solution piece in my hand, but each time I tried to fit it in place, the light was blocked and I was left in an unbearable empty darkness. I removed the piece, and tried repeatedly to make it fit and still have light. I failed in new ways every time. I could not solve this puzzle without losing the light.

Each morning I woke up disturbed—frustrated that I had failed again. Each night I dreaded the return of the dream, and yet desperately ached to find a solution.

Crossing the Hudson

I built the meditation pond ten years ago when we moved in. All those years I meditated, watched the fish swim, and wrote my confessions and insights in a journal. Next month we'll move, and there is little time left for me to use it.

Building the pond was not a small thing. This is because I have no skills. Some men are good with their hands, but not me. I didn't inherit the "handy" gene from my father. The only real skill I have is listening. I have a sign in my office that reads: *Two Ears: No Waiting.*

I'm a psychologist.

The pond is small, maybe only ten by eight feet. But it took me three months of reading, digging, moving stones, fitting liners, repairing leaks, reading some more, cursing, removing the stones, replacing the liners, and fighting the algae. Once it was ready, I went to the local pond-supply house and stocked it with goldfish, koi, and tadpoles. The goldfish, to my surprise, have lived the longest: I meditate as I watch them swim.

It is early fall, and the leaves are beginning to turn. We are moving again. After ten years in our home in Holmdel, New Jersey, we are relocating twenty-two miles south to the Jersey Shore. The interest rates would never again be this favorable, and the opportunity to live by the beach was irresistible. We had moved to Holmdel because of its school system, and now that our daughter, Devon, was in college we decided to make the change. But our combined accrual of possessions was daunting. Much needed to be thrown out.

Each of us took on the task of sorting through the critical mass of our own belongings. For me, the first to go was my wretched collection of sneakers. In more than thirty years of running, I had never thrown any away. This is not to say that some of them hadn't found their way to the garbage. But I had never done the deed. My wife, Nancy, then later, Devon, would periodically thin out the herd by euthanizing the most feeble pair they came across. It might be weeks before I'd realize my loss.

"Nancy, have you seen my blue-and-white Nikes with the ripped heel and busted shoestrings?"

No answer.

"Nancy, did you hear me?"

"Yes, I did," she would say in a matter-of-fact tone.

"I see."

There would then be the obligatory moment of silence for the departed pair of sneakers.

But now we were moving. It was time to jettison all things unused. I came across the sneakers I'd run my first marathon in. I held them in my hand one last time.

Devon was just born. I am training with my friend Bruce for the marathon. Every weekend we do a long run together and chatter away about our problems and dreams. No matter what we talk about we always talk about "The Wall" and wonder what it will be like when we hit it.

I feel the sting of tears fill up my eyes. Cancer took his life last year. My running buddy is gone.

The rubber on the sneakers has disintegrated, and the dried, brittle shoelaces have come apart in several places. After holding them mindfully for a moment, I placed the sneakers at the bottom of a large green Hefty bag. Moments later the bag was filled with sneakers of lesser status; in the end, twenty-eight pairs and two strays.

One idea I'd heard of was to go through all your clothes and label them one through ten. One for those you use often, ten for those you can't recall ever wearing. After this exercise, I donated 80 percent of my clothing. Everything left fit in one wardrobe box. In searching through the hanging clothes and piles of sweaters and T-shirts and socks, I found a stash of some of Devon's stuffed animals. Raggedy Ann (one of Devon's favorites), who now looked more like her name, and a misshapen whale whose name I've forgotten were part of an elite collection that had survived. These would, of course, be spared the fate of the Hefty bag, and I found a clear plastic bin to store all of her stuffed animals and dolls.

I also threw out unlabeled videotapes; CDs of music I didn't like or listen to anymore; cheap, crummy tools; and every graduate psychology paper I'd written. Hundreds of outdated textbooks and dozens worn beyond their usefulness were pitched. In all, twenty cartons of books were tossed and eight boxes donated to a literacy program.

A box of keys, perhaps four dozen or so, had collected in a kitchen drawer. Except for a few, none were labeled. I dumped the box into the garbage, keeping only the ones with tags.

The first was a small key that had my father-in-law's handwritten inscription on the tag that read "Back Screen Door." I knew we would need it for his shore house in Lavollette, and I put it up on the counter. The second one was marked "shed," which I knew I had labeled. It was a spare key to the lock on our garden shed, and I made a mental note to leave it for the new owners. The third key was larger and pointier than the others: the round key tag read, "360 Honda."

I am riding on my motorcycle to teach my psychology class. A red cardinal swoops down, crashes into my leg, and explodes on impact. I sold the motorcycle that weekend and have never ridden one since.

I fondled the key between my fingers and stuck it in my pocket.

I sold off the Ping-Pong and pool tables, the wheelbarrow, the antique glasses, and the 1950s red vinyl and chrome kitchen chair. I gave away my old TV, and every old computer part was thrown out.

In the den closet a hodgepodge of stuff had collected over the years. Boxes of photographs, research videos, and a collection of plays I had studied while on my fellowship at Princeton. Most of these things were keepers, but a box shoved on the top bookshelf had no labels or markings. I hadn't a clue what it contained.

Finally, there was only the one carton left, so I got a small stepladder and took it down. It was larger and heavier than I had anticipated and covered with dust. I stepped down the ladder and placed it on the floor. On the top of the box, in my sister's handwriting, were three letters.

MOM

A shudder of recognition went through me. My sister, Donna, had been the one who took care of the details at the condo in Florida after my mother died. She sold things off, packed things up, and managed the details of the funeral. This box had everything she thought I should have from Mom. She shipped it up the month after the funeral, and I immediately put it up in the corner of the closet. It had been sitting there unopened for three years.

My first impulse was to leave it untouched, my curiosity tempered by self-protection. Obviously I'd been resisting the impulse to open the box for years. I convinced myself that there were more important things to do than to mull over its contents, so I pushed it over into the corner of the room and made myself busy with cleaning the closet's floor and shelves.

The box of photographs I had taken out was old, and the sides bulging and weak. There were shopping bags full of photos and negatives that had never been sorted. The photo albums had pictures falling out of them, and the last thing I wanted to do was take time to go through them all. I decided to get a new, bigger box, tape it up, and put in everything for a future organizing fest.

With the new box assembled I began stacking the albums inside it. I resisted the temptation to open the first three, but there were photos hanging out of the fourth one, preventing it from closing.

A stack of old four-by-four-inch black-and-white photos of Devon's birth were jammed inside. I had a dim recollection of wanting to put together a collection of photos from my childhood and Nancy's to add to Devon's to pass on to her someday. I found a color photo of the last time my father held Devon, and black-and-white photos from my third birthday party at my grandmother's summer bungalow in Edgewater. I thumbed through them with the intention of simply putting a rubber band around them and moving on. Then I saw the picture of Gary, my cousin, and me in my red wagon when we were kids. I held the photograph in my hands and studied our broad, infectious smiles. There were no two happier kids on the planet.

I am at Gary's funeral, my father's, then Steve's.

Every photo provides a drift into reverie. I remember the cake at the birthday party, the hats, Gary. I am lost in half dreams and memories. How did this happen? How do two kids start out so happy and . . . ?

Another color photograph wedged in with the black-and-whites caught my attention. It was a photo I'd taken of Devon's umbilical cord still attached. As I pulled the snapshot from the pile, other photographs of her birth were exposed: photos of the nurses in the delivery room, of Nancy holding Devon, and a picture of a disheveled, disoriented me as proud papa.

They have locked me in the rubber room in the psychiatric wing of the hospital.

The box from my mother seems to tug at me from across the room. The lure is too great, and I leave the photo box and rip back the packing tape to open the top flaps. A copy of the note my father had left for me just before his death, along with a copy of the note he left for Donna and the original to my mother were on the very top of the box. My sister had clipped them together with a note that said these were on Mom's bedside table the night she died.

More photos, much older than the ones across the room, are underneath the letters. I've never seen these before. They are from my mother's bridal shower: many sour faces, with the Irish and the Italians in separate photos. In the photo of the Irish delegation my aunt sits with a cigarette wedged between her fingers. The black-and-white photos are the perfect format; it is hard to imagine these people in color.

There are more photos, stray documents, and a box of notes that look like the beginning of a diary. The notes were written on several yellow pads and loose white lined paper. The writing was my mother's, but it was difficult to read. Her handwriting was shaky and the papers not paginated. I decided not to sort through them now, and bundled them into a folder.

There was an old 8 mm camera my father used to have, some name tags from his union days as a journeyman electrician, and coins from foreign countries mixed in a small white box with several of my dad's guitar picks.

My father is sitting on a guitar amp playing Chuck Berry while I am dancing. I am ten years old.

Wrapped in the bottom of the box were a few small oil paintings my mother had created while taking classes. The paintings, all still lifes, were actually quite good: my mother the artist, sensitive and creative. This was a side of her I'd never seen while growing up.

A small roll of tissue was in the bottom of the box: toilet paper, it seemed, rolled and flattened into one of the corners. My curiosity got the best of me, and I reached down to pick it up; it was heavier than you might imagine something that size could be. I unrolled the tissue layer by layer until the object was revealed. Here, at the bottom of my mother's treasures, was a cigarette lighter.

My father's name, *Artie*, was inscribed on the bottom.

I am staring at the white sheet covering his body.

⌒

His nose was broken from the fall. A purple-blue orb had swollen over his right eye; there was a deep cut through his upper lip where his teeth had come through. The rest of my father's body was naked under the thin sheet with its dry creases making it seem more like paper than cloth. I remember thinking how cold it was in the room and how little protection the sheet offered. But his body wasn't warm anymore. It seemed ironic that, when I was in college, he moved with my mother and sister from New Jersey to Florida to get away from the cold.

He was dead before he hit the ground. The heart attack had been so sudden he didn't have time to put his arms up to protect his face. Walking alongside a neighbor's house, he apparently fell to his knees and then face first into the lawn with his hands by his sides. I never knew a heart attack could drop someone midstep. Grass stains on the knees of his pants, his broken nose, and the cut lip confirmed the doctor's assumption. It was three hours before the neighbor found him.

The medical examiner looked like a chubby kid with a gray wig plopped on his head to make him seem older. He saw me standing in front of my father's gurney. "If you gotta go," he said, "this is the fastest way. No pain, no suffering. We should all be so lucky." He also said how young my father looked for a man of sixty. My mother and sister walked in as the examiner finished talking. They had already seen Dad and had given me a moment to be with him.

After the first heart attack at age forty-nine, his doctor told him he could never smoke again. After thirty years, he stopped his three-pack-a-day habit, and for the first time in his life he was able to lose eighty pounds, exercise regularly, and eat in moderation. For the last eleven years he did everything he could to improve his life. The survival rate for his myocardial infarction was less than 7 percent after five years, and virtually zero after ten. His making it to sixty was nothing short of a miracle, but the suddenness of his death caught us all off guard.

The doctor explained the paperwork that comes with dying. He described the forms my mother would have to sign, and the procedures necessary to release the body to the funeral home. As he spoke he handed her two large gray plastic envelopes. One contained my father's clothes and shoes, the other his personal effects. I took the bag with my father's clothes; my mother took the other. As she opened it, her eyes drifted off toward the left, and the doctor went on about how to get copies of death certificates, who to send them to, and how good my father looked. But her mind was somewhere else. I had heard the story so many times. I knew what she was thinking.

She remembered the wind. It pushed hard against the ferry, making the fifteen-minute trip from Edgewater to Manhattan seem longer. Like a stream that parts around a rock, the breeze surrounded, then passed by the boat. It was only 8:30 in the morning and already 82 degrees. Another hot August day. The veteran smokers moved toward the back of the boat.

She cupped her hands to protect the flame. Failing twice, she removed the unlit Chesterfield from her lips. He watched from across the open door of the main cabin, and after the second flame blew out, he moved toward her. At five foot eleven and nearly three hundred pounds, his presence not only blocked the wind, but offered a formidable sense of protection. Somehow his standing close, his smell, his smile, his calm blue eyes, and wavy black hair all made her feel safe.

In one move his right hand snapped open a heavy silver-and-gold lighter. The top of it arched back, and, with a smooth swipe of his thumb along the flint wheel, a broad low flame was ignited. He held it close enough for her to lean in, and she returned the Chesterfield to her lips.

She took a deep drag on the cigarette. She wanted it to light and drew the burn back further than necessary. "Would he notice this?" she wondered. In a reflex she touched the tip of her tongue to the filter allowing her to inhale, but it was too much. Every pore seemed to fill with smoke, and her lungs inflated until her eyes watered. Fearing an unattractive cough, she pressed her lips together hard and gave the weakest, strangest smile to hide her condition. Instead of sultry or sensual, she looked seriously ill. This man had literally taken her breath away.

He had noticed how deep her draw was, and a tight smile of temporary power pulled on the corner of his mouth. It disappeared quickly, and he closed the lighter with the same smooth style. A half flick of his wrist, and the hinged cap snapped into place. With his Camel to the left side of his mouth, he dropped the lighter back into his pants pocket. As if some grand choreographer had arranged it, the sun conspired with a wisp of smoke from his cigarette and forced him to shut his eyes and turn his head. This was her chance: as he spun away she coughed once and blew every last bit of smoke up into the swirling wind. He turned back, just in time to see her smile. He smiled back, but looked past her to the emerging view of the New York skyline. The boat ride was more than half over. Soon they would dock, and his chance to make the most of a breezy August morning would be gone.

"Do you believe this wind?"

"I'm surprised your lighter didn't go out," she said.

"It's windproof. I got it when I was in the navy, in Panama."

He took it back out of his pocket.

"Here, feel it," he said.

She held out her left hand, and as he reached to give it to her, the tips of his fingers brushed the outside edge of her palm. Her hand squeezed together and her thumb pulled in tight to make a shallow space to receive the lighter. He placed it, and with a deliberate pause let his hand stay a half second longer than it should. She didn't allow herself to meet his eyes, but knew what he had done and that he was looking at her. He moved his hand back and in that moment let the Panama trinket speak for him. She took it in her hand and moved it up and down a few times. Finally, she decided to say something about the weight.

"That's amazing."

"You don't find stuff like that in the States," he said.

"Thank you for bringing it all the way from Panama to help me out."

"I couldn't just let you go through a book of matches."

She placed her thumb along its side and extended her arm to return it.

"Thanks for the light, and letting me see it; it's beautiful," she said.

"Why don't you keep it?"

He was surprised at his own words. It was as though someone else had spoken. He felt a little outside of himself, unsure of what would happen next.

She pushed the lighter toward him and finally looked him in the eyes.

"I can't take this!" she said.

"Well, how about I loan it to you?"

"Oh no, no! I can't take this!" *She found herself smiling and refusing at the same time.* "Here, take it. It's yours, from Panama, from the navy. I don't even know your name."

"It's on the lighter."

She stopped and pulled it back, turning it in her hand.

"I don't see anything on here." She said, "Is it engraved?"

"Yeah, take a look."

She looked at the gold ribbed bar running down the middle of the silver case. It was simple, intriguing, and elegant.

"I don't see anything," she said.

"On the bottom," he said as he pointed.

She moved the lighter to her other hand and focused on the flat metal surface. Etched in cursive writing in lowercase letters was his name.

"Artie!" she said. She smiled and looked right at him.

"Artie Tomasulo," he said. "Pleased to meet you."

He put the Camel back in his mouth and stuck out his right hand. She transferred the lighter from one hand to the other and held out hers. They shook hands like two kids who just agreed to split the profits of their lemonade stand. It seemed comical to them both. Somehow they were already more intimate than a handshake.

"Now you have to show me something with your name on it," he said.

She was drawn to him, but knew the objections her family would have. Everything about Artie was Italian; his hair, his complexion, his manner. She could hear the vowel roll off the end of his name and into her father's mouth. There it would get ground up in Gaelic and spewed out as worthless, tasteless spit. She could see and hear her father's rage. Maybe he would smash a mirror or smack her across the face. Maybe he would get drunk and come looking for him as he had done with other boyfriends. She needed someone to protect her, someone who would treat her better than her family. She didn't want to be living at home anymore. At twenty-two, her dark curly hair, bright blue eyes, and solid breasts guaranteed weekend dates, but they were all boys, and she wanted something more. Someone who made her feel safe, feel loved. Someone very different from her parents.

Her eyes suddenly snapped back from their fixed gaze, and she bundled the gray bag under her arm. She managed a "thank you" to the doctor, and as she turned to leave, he encouraged her to make a list of everyone to contact. She nodded knowingly, and a red thread of memory stretched back to that August in 1947. Her family was Irish, and his

Italian. Both hated the fact they were dating. She recalled her parents'
warning, "Don't marry a guinea," and heard her brother and sister advis-
ing, "All those wops are in the Mafia." It was no better on his side. His
mother made it clear that food was the yardstick by which to measure
promise. "Irish girls can't cook," she said, and, "Italian boys should be
with their own kind." His father only knew how to shrug and never in-
terfered with his wife's opinion. It never got any better, and the families
marinated themselves in their respective bitterness for decades. It was a
battle that now had literally lasted a lifetime.

"I don't have anything with my name on it," she lied.

*Her underwear was marked in pen with her first name. Even at twenty-
two she still had to keep her sister from stealing her things, but she wouldn't
allow herself to say it. It was too suggestive, too forward. She had already
imagined the whole dialogue that would have followed, and it was too pro-
vocative for her to consider. It was better, much better, to lie.*

*"You must have something with your name on it. An ID, or license?"
he said.*

"Sure, I have my ID, but I don't drive; no one in my family drives."

*She rooted around in her straw pocketbook. Why hadn't she taken the
dark brown one with the leather edges? It looked so much better! Oh God!
She just told him that no one in the family drives—now he knows everyone
in her family is a drunk. She wanted to tell him she was different, she was
nothing like her family. Could he tell? Did he know already how crazy
they were?*

"Here's my ID," she said.

He took it in his hand and read it out loud:

*"Margaret Henry," he said. "It's a good name. You like being called
Margaret?"*

"I like Marge, or Margie."

"Well, Margie," he said, "what time do you take the ferry back tonight?"

Something in Artie gave her hope. "Six-thirty," she said.

*"Why don't you hang on to the lighter until then? I'll meet you right here,
at six-thirty, right in the back of the boat."*

A stream of tears had been falling down her face since she closed the bag. She no longer made an attempt to wipe her pain away. In the last twelve hours she had cried so much she'd lost track of when she was crying and when she wasn't. After thirty-seven years together, what was she going to do? Thirty-seven years of plans, and dreams, and coffee. Walking, laughing, smoking, and preparing parties. The habits of being in love, the comfort and luxury of routine—all of it gone. The war between their families made their bond all the more important. What was she going to do now?

All day long she held on to the lighter. He was right; you couldn't find something like this in the States. Her job was boring, but filing papers for an insurance company never really bothered her, except today. She held the lighter in one hand, then the other, turning it over, feeling its smoothness, its character, its weight. She would see his name on the bottom, and nothing but possibilities bubbled up in her head. Was he the one? Where would they live? What would the kids look like?

My mother, sister, and I drove back to my parents' home. The furniture seemed lonely and depressed. The couch, where my father sat to read his books and watch TV, now seemed out of place, not part of the furniture anymore. He was gone, and the furniture knew it.

My mother laid the gray bag down on the counter and busied herself making a pot of coffee. She had never liked the Mr. Coffee machine I bought for them years ago. Mom slipped into the familiar routine of taking the coffeepot out from under the counter, filling the inner basket with six scoops of Chock full o'Nuts, and eyeing the water level as the pot filled with tap water. Suddenly, she was crying again. She put the pot down on the counter and cried into her hands. With her hands still covering her eyes, she took one deep breath, then another. She dropped her hands, stared at the coffeepot, then finally picked it up and poured half the water down the sink. One by one she scooped half the coffee back into the Chock full o'Nuts can.

At 6:15 she was already down by the boat slip. The temperature hit 97, and the sweat from her own body was unbearable. The morning breeze had gone, and the hazy stillness made even breathing difficult. She wondered if her name on her underwear might run. She looked around but didn't see him,

and as the throng jostled onto the boat she made her way back to the same
spot where she had been in the morning.

When she got to the back of the boat, she took a Chesterfield out of the straw
pocketbook and decided to give the lighter a try. She had seen him strike it
flawlessly, but didn't think she could do it with the same style. She held the
bottom of it with her right hand and, as if she were removing the top part
of a shell from a hard-boiled egg, she opened the lighter. What a solid feel it
had! She grazed her thumb along the flint wheel, but it didn't have the quick-
ness needed for a good spark. It was harder to push than other lighters she
had used. She tried it again, then again. Thinking the wick might need some
fluid, she turned the lighter upside down and moved it up and down like a
ketchup bottle.

"That's quite a technique you've got there," said a familiar voice.

"How did you do that so easy?" she said. She smiled as she handed it back
to him.

"It's all in the wrist."

With a bit of showmanship he repeated the same graceful movement from
that morning. She drew the burn back on the cigarette, this time being care-
ful not to over-inhale.

"Thanks," she said.

"I'm available as a personal cigarette lighter. Every time you need one,
I'm your man."

Her father refused to come to the wedding. It was just as well. The
sour faces, her brother filling his flask from the open bar, and the stupid
ornate "thrones" his mother ordered for her and Artie to sit in made the
day a nightmare. Nothing she had asked for was there. Meatball sandwiches and pasta rather than roast chicken; whiskey at the tables, not
wine; and a band that played the tarantella every time her mother-in-law
was near the dance floor.

The wedding hadn't been the worst of it. The baby shower a year
later at his mother's apartment was a mix of the Irish (her sister, four
cousins, and her mother) and the Italians (her mother-in-law, an aunt,
and Artie's cousin). Within a half hour of their meeting, the Irish delegation stormed out. The four cousins had been asked to put out their

cigarettes because his mother didn't want the apartment to smell like a whorehouse.

"I'm your man."

The ferry started with a lurch. The early evening sun scattered diamond chips on the rippling Hudson, but it wasn't the river they were floating on: they were drifting along on possibilities. The Jersey shoreline more a destiny than destination.

The half-pot of coffee was ready. My sister and I declined, and my mother set out one cup between the sugar and milk pitcher. She poured the coffee and took her time adding one, then a second spoonful of sugar. When this was done she added two dribs of milk and began to stir. The clang of the spoon against the ceramic cup went on without end. She took a sip, picked up the spoon, and the clanging started again.

Finally, she put the spoon back on the counter and with her right hand opened the gray bag. She stared inside it waiting to feel her reaction. After a moment she reached in and found his nitroglycerine pills.

At forty-nine the heart attack had changed everything. Artie had come home from the hospital to find the house amazingly clean. Everything had been scrubbed. She worked hard to prepare his homecoming. He was weak, but at least he was alive. He had never thought he would have a heart attack, certainly not before the age of fifty. The low-sodium diet would change his whole way of living. Everything he put in his mouth was first analyzed for sodium content. The doctor told him if he swallowed two olives together, it could kill him.

But the food was nothing compared to not smoking. He spent three weeks craving cigarettes in the hospital. The physician said it would help him if Margie got the smell of smoke out of the house. She had the rugs, the curtains, and the bedding cleaned. She made sure *everything* was de-contaminated. The counters, the cabinets, the couch—everything was cleaned to perfection. The only place not touched by this purification was the porch. That was where she went to smoke, forty or fifty times a day.

His wallet was the next thing she found in the bag. Photographs of my sister and me as kids, a picture of him and Mom in the Bahamas on their twenty-fifth wedding anniversary, six singles, his driver's license, and his card from the electricians' union. The expiration date had been eleven years earlier.

By the time the ferry was docking in Edgewater, plans had been made to meet at nine o'clock at the front gate to Palisades Amusement Park. Joking, he said he would report for duty with his trusty Panamanian lighter.

In the bottom of the bag there was some change, two sticks of Juicy Fruit gum, the watch he'd bought at a garage sale two weeks before (for a buck), and the lighter. She pulled it from the bag and held it in front of her with both hands. She ran her thumbs back and forth along the edges, feeling the smoothness, the coldness. Artie was never without it. "I never know," he used to say, "when you might need me to perform my duties."

After a moment she took the lighter and her coffee and walked around the counter toward the sliding-glass doors to the porch. There were calls to be made, but she needed time for herself and went out to the porch, shutting the glass doors behind her. Sitting on one of the white plastic chairs, she placed her coffee cup on the round table in front of her and picked up the half-empty pack of Chesterfields. She drew one out, put it in her mouth, and flicked back the cap of the lighter.

Saturday

My father was a spy, a double agent for the CIA and the FBI. To conceal his identity from foreign agents, he worked as an electrician for Lever Brothers Company. He had all kinds of neat tools and gadgets that he said were electrician gear, but I knew they were for defusing bombs, hot-wiring cars, and planting wire taps. This was an excellent disguise for a man of his skill and talent. He never talked about it. We never spoke about his missions, but I am sure he was in demand all over the world. When he was on an assignment, the secret code he would give to Mom was that he was working a double. That meant that he would go into work at eight o'clock in the morning, work eight hours, then stay there for another eight hours and come home at midnight. The cover story was that this would double the amount of time he was going to work at the soap factory. What it really meant was that he was a double agent. He was probably going to protect a foreign ambassador, or maybe steal some secret documents. He might even have to stop an assassin from killing the president.

Dad worked two or three doubles a week. Mom said it was because we needed the extra money, but I knew that wasn't it. Sure, we lived on the top floor of a five-story walk-up apartment building, but my father was a spy for the government, and that meant we could live anywhere in the world. It was just that his undercover work was so important that we had to live where he couldn't be detected. Apparently Dad had been on this assignment since I was born.

Dad worked hard at his job. He left early in the morning, and I would get up to just be with him when he was leaving. I wanted to be around him. He was quiet most of the time. I was not. I asked him a lot of questions while he was getting ready.

"Hey, Dad. Were you on any special assignments this week? Were you, Dad? Did you have to kill any bad guys this week? Hey, Dad, can I go with you on one of your assignments? I won't be any trouble. I just want to blow up a boat or something. I mean, you could wire it and set the bombs and everything. Can I go with you? I'll just press the button and blow it up. Or do you have one of those handle things you push down into a box to blow it up? Can I, Dad? Can I?"

My dad was standing in front of the refrigerator. As he put the sandwich and two apples into his steel lunch box, his neon blue eyes and dark bushy eyebrows kept me under observation. (The lunch box had a secret compartment, but I could never find it.) I could see the corner of my father's mouth stretch into a smile. He looked like a secret agent. His black wavy hair was always combed back, and he seemed to have a permanent tan. My mom said that was because he was Italian, but I think the government probably gave him time off on some island. He was in great shape, strong, tall, and quick. He told me he was a lot heavier when he was younger, but I think he was just trying to make me feel better. I was a fat kid, and he wanted me to know that that wouldn't stop me from being a double agent someday, too.

"Don't you have to go to school today?" he said.

"Sure I do. I figured that we could do it this morning before school. Kill some bad guys or something. Then I could go to school. Mrs. Rogers won't care if I'm late a few minutes. I could tell her we were in a car accident or something. If you don't want me to lie I guess you could write a note to her. 'Dear Mrs. Rogers, please excuse Danny from first grade today. He was helping me on my job and had to kill some bad guys. Thank you, Danny's father.'"

"Danny?"

"Yes, Dad?"

"You have a very active imagination."

"Does that mean I can go to work with you today?"

"Not today."

"Tomorrow then? Can I go to work with you tomorrow?"

"Tomorrow's Saturday."

"You usually work on Saturdays, right, Dad? You get up early and work Saturdays, too. Can I go with you to work tomorrow?"

"Actually I am not working tomorrow."

"No special assignments? No, you know, *doubles*, tomorrow?"

"No, I am just going to relax tomorrow and paint the hallway."

"Hey, Dad, I could help you paint the hallway. I won't be any trouble. I'll just help you roll the paint on the walls. Can I use a mop to put the paint on? It'll go on faster, then maybe we can play a game of Monopoly. So, can I help you paint the hallway tomorrow?"

"How about we go to the park tomorrow?"

"Do you mean it!? You'll go to the park with me tomorrow? Can I wear my Hopalong Cassidy cowboy suit? Let's get up early. I can be ready by six o'clock. Hey, Dad, what do you want to go on first? Do you want to go on the merry-go-round? I bet I can make it spin so fast that you'll fall right off. My friend Kevin and I take turns spinning each other real fast, and we keep going until one of us falls off."

"Don't you get hurt doing that?"

"I only tear my shirt and stuff. I'm pretty good when I fall off. I learned how to roll. I can teach you how to roll, Dad. But I bet you know how to do that already. Do they teach you how to jump out of moving cars and that kind of stuff? Maybe you can teach me how to roll better. Mom really doesn't like it when I come in, and my shirt is ripped."

"Well, let's not go too early. I am working a double tonight, so I don't want to get up too early."

"Sure, Dad. I'll get up early and get my Hopalong Cassidy suit on and wait for you to get up. I'm going to get some caps for my gun. I'll be ready when you get up, Dad. That'll be great. So, we'll play there all morning, and then can we go fishing? I betcha I can catch a big fish like you did last time you went out with the guys down the Hudson. Can we go fishing after the park?"

"We'll see."

"We'll see" was my dad's way of telling me I had asked too many questions. He packed his lunch and got ready to leave. The deal was that I would walk him all the way down the five flights of stairs. Then, just before the last flight of stairs, he would give me a big hug, and I would walk back up to the apartment. It was neat to know that Dad and I had done all this talking and walking every morning before Mom was even awake.

On Saturday mornings I had a ritual of laying out my Hopalong Cassidy cowboy suit with boots, a six-shooter, and a holster. I had a black-and-silver cowboy hat and a black-and-white scarf to go with the outfit. Usually I would get up early and practice my quick draw. Three times out of five I would grab the gun only enough to pull it out of the holster, and it would fall on the floor. Our downstairs neighbors really didn't like when I practiced my quick draw. Kevin, my best friend, and his family lived right below us. Kevin's father, Frank, came up to complain one morning after I had dropped the gun seven times. I think he was pretty mad when I opened the door.

"What the hell are you doing?" he demanded.

"Practicing my quick draw," I said.

"Do you know what time it is?"

"Yes, it's six o'clock," I said proudly.

He didn't even think I was old enough to tell time.

"Don't you know that people are sleeping!" he screamed.

"Not everybody."

"Who the hell is up at this time on a Saturday morning?"

"You're up."

"*You* woke me up!"

"I'm sorry. I'll practice my quick draw near the bed so it won't make noise."

"Goddamn kid." Frank turned his back on me and waved his hand over his shoulder in disgust. He was a skinny little guy who seemed angry all the time. Mom said he was that way because he probably didn't get enough sleep.

I was so excited that Dad and I were going to the park that it was hard for me to concentrate in school. Whenever the teacher called on me, I was daydreaming about all the possibilities. Playing with my dad in the park was something that had never happened before.

Saturday was going to be a great day.

By 6 a.m. I was completely dressed in my Hopalong Cassidy suit and standing over my father's side of the bed, watching him snore. I stood there motionless for about ten minutes, then decided to practice my quick draw. Luckily I pulled the gun out without dropping it. I decided not to tempt fate and kept my gun out of the holster. For the next hour I shot everything in the room six times. I had my special silencer on; Mom and Dad were out like lights, and I knew better than to wake them. I just wanted to be ready to go when Dad got up. I figured if I was right there when he woke up, we could get to the playground faster. Then at 7:03 the unthinkable happened. The phone rang.

With the instincts of the son of a double agent, I turned to the phone on my dad's side of the bed and shot it, silencer off, four times. The smell of the cap-gunpowder went right up my nose and made my eyes blink. Between the phone ringing and the gun shooting, and me dressed for sport, my dad went from a dead sleep to three feet off the bed with a huge yelp. His laser reflexes were in full swing that morning. You could tell he was a double agent, all right. In the blink of an eye he grabbed my gun, yelled something I was never allowed to repeat, picked up the phone, and screamed "hello" into it. I was very impressed.

"Hello? . . . yeah, yeah . . . no, it's fine . . . no, I wasn't sleeping . . . well, anyway I'm up now . . . yeah, I worked a double last night . . . sure . . . go ahead . . . oh, really? . . . you want me to come in . . . right . . . and work a double today . . . eight this morning until midnight tonight. Double time for the whole day . . . wow . . . great . . . no . . . no . . . did I have any plans?"

At this point my father looked at me. I stood there motionless, wide eyed, my six-shooter hanging out. He smiled and glanced over at Mom, who hadn't moved an inch during the whole episode.

"Yeah, Louie, thanks for thinking of me for today, but I have some plans I can't change. Yeah . . . in fact, if you called ten minutes later I would have been gone . . . Yeah, I know it's a lot of money to pass up . . . Yeah, I know, almost a full week's worth of pay for a day's work . . . but what I'm doing is more important than any of that . . . I've got to do it today . . . but thanks for thinking of me and I'll take you up on it an-other time."

He hung up the phone.

Then he grabbed two bottles of Coke and two chicken legs from the refrigerator. By eight o'clock we had consumed the chicken and the soda and went on to have the greatest day ever. We spent the whole day in the park, swinging on the swings, playing ball, shooting it out as cowboys and Indians, and trying to spin one another off the merry-go-round. Dad even bought the Super Deluxe Glider with the extralong rubber band for the propeller. We must have taken half an hour to twist the rubber band up so the plane would fly forever. When we launched it as the grand finale for the day, it sailed over our apartment building for parts unknown. It flew higher and farther than anything I'd ever seen, then disappeared over the rooftop. It was one beautiful, excellent, fan-tastic flight.

⟋

The day after my father died my wife, Nancy, Devon, and I flew down to Florida. Devon was just nine months old. We stayed with my mom for a few days and helped her and my sister clean out the closets. At the bot-tom of most of the closets were the usual things—stray socks, loose change, extra pens, paper clips, a few packets of Sweet'N Low, and some mysterious dust balls. Dad had said that since people "came from dust" and "returned to dust," a dust ball was either somebody coming or going. Between the tears we would give ourselves some relief by saying that the dust balls were probably Dad coming back to check up on us. In each closet I moved Dad's clothes around. As I touched them I could still smell him in the fabric, a small consolation for the pain. At the bottom of one closet was something different from the usual debris: a brown accordion classification folder marked "Don't open until dead." My dad knew how to make a point.

Inside the folder were newspaper clippings, photographs, cards, graduation announcements, and matches from weddings: it was a treasure chest of memorabilia. My dad had saved something from every important event in my sister's life and mine. It was an incredible collection. Some of the stuff was marked with notes, such as "Danny's Junior Prom," and some of it, like the photograph of me in a Nehru jacket flashing the peace sign, needed no explanation. In the bottom of this folder were three separate, small white envelopes, one for each of us: Mom, my sister, and me.

In my envelope was a photograph Mom had taken of Dad and me when I was five or six, and a note in my father's hand that said he had worked too hard and too often when I was growing up. In his own words he told me he loved me and was proud of me, and now that I was a father, he didn't want me to make the same mistake with my daughter that he had made with me. He said he had left something in the attic for me to share with Devon someday. I pulled down the folding stairs to the attic, climbed up, and found a package wrapped in plain paper marked "Danny." I knew what was in it before even picking it up: a brand-new, impact-resistant Super Deluxe Glider.

A Day at the Beach

I loved Palisades Amusement Park. It had the world's largest saltwater pool with waterfalls and waves. My father would take me into the water for as long as I wanted. We would swim under the falling water and get knocked around pretty good. Then we'd play tag until we could barely drag our prune-skinned bodies out of the water and back to the towel. Mom would be right there where we'd left her a couple of hours ago. She'd have on a straw hat that totally covered her head, her ears, and the back of her neck. She would sport huge black sunglasses over the thick white cream cheese smeared on her nose.

Nylon socks completed her outfit.

"The sun," my mom would say, "is the enemy." She didn't enjoy the beach, the people, the noise, the rides, or the lights. It seemed as if everything I liked she hated. I thought the cotton candy and foot-long hot dogs were the greatest. She said they were disgusting, and that the food *and* the people who worked there were greasy. The amusement park had some great stuff: flashlights in the shape of fish and pillows made to look like cans of soup. When I told her how cool I thought they were, all she would say was *ridiculous*.

But my mom never really complained. What I mean to say is that she never actually used words. Her face would look as if she had been chewing lemons and grapefruit all afternoon. Whatever she was feeling simply oozed out of her. I was used to it, but I noticed that other kids stayed away from her. When my mother had the lemon face, even babies avoided her. Kids would be playing in the sand next to her, and when they got too close, it was as though they had suddenly started receiving a radio signal declaring:

"GET AWAY FROM THE BLANKET.

YOU ARE TOO CLOSE TO THE BLANKET.

STAND AWAY FROM THE LADY WITH CREAM CHEESE ON HER FACE."

And the children would move. Children were more sensitive to this radio frequency than adults. Adults knew there was something wrong, but they couldn't quite figure it out. Kids got the message loud and clear. One couple with a three-year-old boy put their blanket too close to ours. My mother never said or did anything, but after a few minutes of picking up signals from my mom, the little boy just stood up and started dragging the blanket toward the pool. "Where are you going?" said his mom. "Bye, bye," was all he said.

A hug from my mother was like cheap ice cream. I wanted it until I got it, then I was disappointed. She loved Dad and me, I'm sure, but sometimes it was hard to tell. The absolute worst thing my dad or I could do was get Mom angry. We would do anything to avoid that. Once my mom got angry, there was no fixing it. "Keeping your mother happy," my dad would say, "is the only thing that really matters."

After we dried off, we'd walk through the park to the car. You couldn't get to the pool without walking through the park, and there was just too much good stuff around. Cotton candy, candy apples, popcorn, rides, cotton candy, the roller coaster, cotton candy, and the games. There were lots of games where you could spin a wheel or throw a ball to win something. The goldfish game fascinated me, but we always seemed to whisk right by it. In big bold pink letters it read, "FISH TOSS." All you had to do was throw a Ping-Pong ball into the fishbowl, and you could win a goldfish. I had always wanted to try it, but it seemed impossible. The tops of the fishbowls were small and the bowls themselves were more than ten feet away. Yet, with a simple throw, I could be a winner. Three balls, one dime, one bowl, one goldfish.

I knew it was a long shot, but as we were walking out on this particular day, I really wanted to win a goldfish. I knew better than to start up with my mother, so I started working on Dad.

"Dad, can I try to win a goldfish, Dad? I'm pretty good at throwing things. I bet you I can do it—what do you say, Dad? Can I try it?"

My mom (who never carried *anything* to or from the pool) didn't even let my dad talk.

"Goldfish are the dirtiest animals in existence," she said. "All you have to do is see how a goldfish moves, and you realize it's filthy." (My mom had said nearly the same thing about a woman dressed in gold stretch pants and a red blouse we had seen in New York a few weeks earlier.)

"I don't want a dirty smelly fish in my house. Do you hear me? Look at me. *Look at me,*" she said to me. "I don't want any part of this thing. I won't allow you to bring it home, so don't waste your time trying."

My mother's icy blue eyes seemed to burn me when she was mad. I don't know why exactly, but I started to cry. Crying made me lose any words I might have had, and I stood in front of the Fish Toss rubbing my eyes.

My mom and dad had one of their conferences. Actually, those conferences were more of my mother talking and my father nodding his head and shrugging his shoulders. This time it was quick. My dad explained something to my mom that seemed to calm her down. He came over to me and said, "Why don't you give it a try? If it goes in, you can keep the goldfish."

I remember really hearing the words, *if it goes in,* in a special way. The words jumped out at me, and I realized right then and there that my parents were banking on me screwing up. They'd let me throw the balls, miss, then go home without a fuss. That way the failure would be on my shoulders. I couldn't blame them because they had let me throw the balls. My mother wouldn't have to be the bad guy, and my father would have given me the chance. It would all be on me. I was trapped.

I wiped away my tears and stepped up to the Fish Toss. My father gave the guy behind the stand a dime, and I was handed three Ping-Pong balls. In my head there were only two words to describe what I felt. *This sucks.* I tried to focus my eyes on the fishbowls. *This sucks. This game sucks. This day sucks. The pool sucks.* Sucks was a new word in my vocabulary.

I stared hard at the bowls. There were six of them spread out on the stand. It wasn't difficult; it was impossible. I wasn't even sure the Ping-Pong ball would fit in the bowls. I was defeated before I began. It was hopeless. My mother had won again, and my father's ploy had left me without his usual support. Tears blurred my vision. Not only could I not see, but now I didn't care. I thought about throwing the balls, but my heart just wasn't in it. I had them all in my hand and was ready to take one to throw when, for some reason I still don't understand, I threw all three balls together. It was an act of desperation and an acknowledgment of defeat. I didn't care about the balls, or the fish, or the amusement park. All I cared about was being angry at my mother—something I wasn't allowed to be. The balls flew in the air and, in a surreal moment, the impossible happened. One of them went in.

Everyone was stunned. Even the guy behind the counter was beside himself. I turned toward my father with a look that almost said, "I'm sorry," and I didn't look at my mother because she wasn't there. She had walked away from the stand to smoke a cigarette. When the guy behind the stand realized what had happened, he bellowed his trademark call. "Aaaaaaanother winner here. Here goes aaaaaaanother winner."

I screamed, a lot. The tears of moments earlier had given way to screams of delight. I jumped up and down and waved my arms wildly in the air. It was all perfectly legal. Despite unbelievable odds, I had won a fish! By the time my mother made her way over to the stand, the man had a goldfish in a plastic bag. Stupid me. I thought you won the gold-fish bowl with the goldfish. No. Just the goldfish and a plastic bag. I was upset by the idea and asked the man behind the counter if he would give me a bowl: "The bowl . . ." he said, ". . . is yours, Sonny, for *three* wins."

I looked at my dad—then my mom. When I turned back to the man behind the counter, the words I had waited long enough to say finally popped out. "That sucks," I said. My father eked out a weak smile, and my mother took off for the car.

We drove back to the apartment in silence. My mother's attitude had become distinctly sour. The lemon-and-grapefruit face returned. She was seething and smoking at a furious pace. There was extraordinary tension between my parents that erupted when we got home. It was as though the goldfish coming into the apartment was the final act of be-trayal for my mother. She screamed that my father shouldn't have let this happen, that I had manipulated the situation, and that her wishes were being ignored. She vowed that she wouldn't allow the fish to stay. The unthinkable had happened: Mom was upset, and all hell was break-ing loose. I put the goldfish in a Mason jar on the windowsill.

The next day was Monday and my father got up and went off to work. I jumped out of bed and ran to look at my goldfish, excited because today was the day I would name him. My mother was ironing and smoking in the kitchen. The fish and the jar were nowhere to be found. When I asked where my goldfish was, my mother said the fish had died, and she had flushed him down the toilet. She didn't look at me and kept iron-ing. I knew she was lying. I went back to my room and began composing my runaway letter. Kindergarten wouldn't begin for another month, so the letter was without the advantage of intelligible words. But it read, in part, "This sucks and I'm running away from home forever."

I packed my Hopalong Cassidy clothes and my Howdy Doody doll and went to eat breakfast while my mother was still ironing. She had cereal in a bowl with a small pitcher of milk waiting for me. I finished it and took an extra banana into my room. The plan was set. When she took her midmorning nap, I'd escape out the front door and down the steps to my grandmother's apartment in New York City. Grandma would be happy to see me. There were hundreds of buses that went by our apartment building. I would just ask the bus driver to take me to Grandma's.

When she lay down on the couch in the living room, I knew it would only be a matter of minutes before she'd drift off. Her snoring was my signal. I gathered my stuff in a paper bag from the A&P and headed for the door. Our apartment was arranged so the living room was down the end of the hallway from the door. She wouldn't be able to see my escape. I struggled with the door, never having opened it myself, but the puzzle was too great to solve. Chains, locks, bolts with pins. I needed a new getaway plan. The fire escape was too high for me, so, in what I think was my first moment of true creative inspiration, Plan B was formed. I would make my exit by way of the dumbwaiter.

I had seen my mother use it many times. The dumbwaiter was in the kitchen, and she would stick the garbage in, close the door, and press the button to send it to the basement. Later, when she got to the basement, she would remove it and throw the garbage into one of the pails. If she was carrying groceries home from the store, she could do the reverse. The dumbwaiter was in the center of the building, and each of the four apartments on every floor had access to it. It was the perfect getaway vehicle. I opened the door, and the dumbwaiter was there. What luck! I didn't have to risk waking her up with the noise of pressing the "up" button to bring it to our floor. I quietly pulled the chair from under the oval kitchen table. The gray-speckled vinyl seat cover matched the tabletop, and I stepped into its soft mounded center. The air in the seat's cushion hissed out, and I held my breath hoping the noise wouldn't wake her. I pulled myself into the dumbwaiter. It was cramped, but I settled in with my A&P bag of runaway clothes, Howdy Doody doll, and banana. In a less awkward move than I expected, I pushed the "down" button and closed the door. Free at last.

It was the darkest place I had ever been, and the smell in the dumbwaiter made breathing optional. I was continually on the verge of throwing up. When I finally stopped in the basement, I realized the door would open only from the outside. The architect of the dumbwaiter had never considered my escape plan. I stayed there for approximately seventy-two million hours.

In the dark, in the smelliest place on earth, I had time to contemplate my options in life. Because I was only five, it was a short list. Immediately I began considering how much more fun it would be to be back in my room, or even back in my bed. My first experience with solitary confinement came to an abrupt end when a neighbor returning with groceries suddenly opened the dumbwaiter door. I ran back up the five floors of stairs and knocked on the front door. My mother opened it. She said simply that she knew I'd be back. She made no fuss, nor any mention of my daring escape. Once I was inside, she locked the door behind me.

⌇

Twenty-five years later I was in the last year of a PhD program in psychology and over the summer I was reading a book entitled *Group and Family Therapy*; it was an overview of the different theories of family pathology and how group therapy can provide a correction. So I was on the beach, early in the morning, reading about family pathology when God figured it would be better for me to *watch* family pathology than read about it.

There were four of them. Each found a corner of the blanket to park.

The mother, mid-thirties, wore a huge white sombrero-style sun hat to match her oversized, white, cover-up beach dress with oversized, black sunglasses. She sat in the far righthand corner of the army-issue green blanket and varnished herself with a number 60 sunblock. To the mother's right was her mother-in-law: a short, ageless, round, Italian grandmother complete with her hair in a bun, pointy eyeglasses, and funeral black bathing suit. To the mother's left, her husband: slicked black hair, smooth deep olive skin, designer sunglasses, flabby belly and hairy chest adorned with a large gold chain. Directly across from the mother was her three-year-old son: slicked black hair, designer sunglasses, flabby belly, hairless chest, no chain. The mother and the mother-in-law went at it constantly. Grandma started them off.

"Did you put mayonnaise on the ham-and-cheese sandwiches?"

"I don't remember. I packed all the food by myself; I can't remember everything."

"You know I hate mayonnaise."

"Eat something else."

"You didn't make *one* sandwich without mayonnaise?"

"There is a lot of food in there. Look around. If you had wanted a particular type of sandwich you should have helped me pack. Then you could have made one for yourself."

"You did this on purpose."

"Don't be ridiculous. Do you think I'm so small minded? I'm not like you. I didn't purposefully plan to forget the pickles and the sandwiches with mustard!"

"There are no pickles?"

And so it would go. The father was buried under three Sunday newspapers, the *New York Times*, the *Daily News*, and the *Asbury Park Press*. The little boy just played in the corner of the blanket and got lost in his own world. It was fun to watch him. He made noises, dug in the sand, and was oblivious to the oddities of his family. The mother and grandmother kept at it until the mother spontaneously stopped talking and looked at her son. With outstretched arms she called across the blanket, "Come give Mommy a kiss! You are so adorable. Come here!"

The boy stood up and began his trek across the blanket toward Mom. The moment he began, his mother screamed at him. "Look what you did to the blanket! Look at the sand you dragged all over it! I told you before to be careful! Get off the blanket!"

With that she pulled his arm and yanked him over to her side. She yelled until she drained the delight out of the boy. The grandmother immediately began to comfort him, telling him not to worry, everything would be all right. Digging deep into the cooler she pulled out a ham-and-cheese sandwich and handed it to him.

"Here you go. Here's a nice ham-and-cheese sandwich with mayonnaise for you. Grandma doesn't like mayonnaise, but that's okay. You have this one. Grandma will find something else to eat."

Like a released hostage, the broken boy returned to his corner and picked up his toys. The grandmother and mother went back to sparring.

"Is the only type of sunblock you brought a number 60?" began the grandmother.

"That's the only type I use."

"Other people might use other types."

"Then *other* people should have brought other types."

"I don't see the ginger ale."

"There isn't any."

"I don't drink Diet Pepsi."

"It won't kill you."

"You really don't like me, do you?"

"Let's just enjoy the beach."

"You don't even like the beach, do you?"

"Why don't you let me get some sun?"

"You Irish people hate the sun. You're so covered up, how could you get any sun on you at all?"

"Just let me relax, okay?"

"I'm not stopping you. All I do is try to help, and what do I get? I don't know why I gave you all that money."

"Oh, please, don't start in with the money again. You gave us ten thousand for the house, and now you live with us. That's not what I call a bargain."

"I'll just have some water. You did bring water, didn't you?"

"I don't remember."

Then it happened again. The mother looked up and saw her boy across from her. Again she called to him. "Come give Mommy a kiss!" The boy was understandably suspicious. He started to get up, thought better of it, then tried to ignore the request, and went back to playing with his toys. His mother turned on the charm and used her outstretched arms and voice to lure the boy toward her. She induced a trance, and again he stepped into the center of the blanket.

This time the mother swatted his behind twice for the crime of trespassing with sandy feet. There she was, live and in-person, the schizo-phrenogenic mother from page 86. She had him in a double bind—he was trapped into a damned-if-you-do, damned-if-you-don't, lose-lose endgame. If he had refused his mother, she would have gotten angry, yet she set him up to do it wrong. Unless he was an emotional genius, he couldn't get it right. He cried, loudly.

The father finally put down his newspaper and lost it. He started screaming at his wife.

"What the hell is going on here! We come all the way down to the Jersey Shore to spend a nice quiet Sunday, and what the hell are you doing? You two are fighting like cats and dogs, and what the hell are you yelling at the kid for? We're at the *fucking* beach for Christ's sake. He's allowed to get a little *fucking* sand on the *fucking* blanket. This is sup-posed to be a fun *fucking* day!"

The wife fired back.

"Mister Big Shot has to shoot his mouth off and let the whole state of New Jersey know our family business. You never even pick your head up from the Goddamn newspaper until you decide it's time to explode. Somebody's got to discipline this boy."

Grandma wasn't one to let an opportunity pass. She pointed her fin-ger like a sword at the mother.

"Look at what you do to everybody. You made your son cry and your husband curse. I didn't raise him that way. That's your doing."

The father told his son to come over to him, and the mother waved the child away. The boy wiped tears from his eyes as his father began reading him the funny papers. The cycle was complete. The father was teaching his son how to cope with the family: stay out of it as long as you can, scream at everyone to get control, then get lost in the funny papers. About twenty minutes later the boy drifted back to his corner. The blanket battlefield had gone silent. Mother busied herself with sun-tan lotion, Grandma rummaged for food, and Dad immersed himself in the stock section of the *Times*. The boy was playing, but not with the same zeal he had before.

To my amazement, two hours have gone by. I have long since abandoned my reading and was somewhat at a loss to explain what kept my interest. Surely I had better things to do than to watch these antics. I was fascinated by a boy who never once said a word. In the whole two hours he never uttered a single sound other than to cry. I realize the only time he was at peace was when he was in his own world—that's when I finally recognized the family.

It was mine.

Confessions of a Former Child

On October 11, 1959, I stopped eating watermelon. By the end of the month I had cut out rye bread, cantaloupe, honeydew melon, all types of apples, Bing cherries, sesame-seeded bagels, tapioca pudding with raisins, and hard-boiled eggs. I had suspicions about chocolate-chip ice cream. My parents wondered why an eight-year-old would restrict his diet in this particular way. On occasion they would ask, and I would lie.

"Not hungry," was all I said.

That would be that. My parents shrugged, I shrugged, and we went about our business. When I turned down my favorite, split-pea soup, Mom gave me a look and asked the question, "Are you all right?"

"Sure, Mom," I lied. "I just don't feel like pea soup today." Blueberry muffins, pasta e fagioli, peanut M&M's, tomatoes, peas, corn, all types of jam, olives, chickpeas, grapes, and button candy followed. By the time Thanksgiving rolled around I had lost three and one-half pounds and was eating mostly cream-cheese-and-butter sandwiches. This was serious. It was all due to my little sister. Well, I didn't know she was my sister. She turned out to be a sister, but how was I supposed to know that? She wasn't even born yet.

Let me explain.

October 11th was a Saturday. I was home playing, and my dad was at work. I missed him. I always hoped Dad and I would do something on Saturday mornings, and I had been looking forward to the day, but he was gone before I woke up. Mom was doing the usual things—cleaning up, then yelling at me for not cleaning up; washing the laundry, then yelling at me for getting stuff dirty; picking my clothes up off the floor, and saying (to no one in particular) that I was "just like your father." Since she had mentioned my father, I decided to ask about him.

"Where's Dad?"

"He's working a double today."

"How come?" I said.

"We're going to need some extra money."

"Why do we need extra money?"

She looked at me for a longer time than she normally did to answer a question. This was the clue I missed. Nothing good follows a long look from your mother. It meant I should change the topic or forget I'd asked the question. Right then I should have realized that there was something bad, strange, or weird about to happen. She kept looking at me and told me to "sit down." The "sit down" command was the ultimate. Someone had died; she had found my report card; or I was in very serious trouble for something yet to be determined. I remember that as I sat down, she sat down, and I noticed that she was, well, there is no nice way to say this, *chunky*. Not really fat, but for the first time I can remember I noticed her belly stuck out, and she was easing herself down into the chair.

I sat across from her. I liked our kitchen table. It was round, but if you put the extra pieces in, it was oval and very sturdy. It was the kind of table you could really lean your elbows on and get comfortable with. That's what I did, as I sat across from her and she talked. My arms were folded underneath my chin. She looked at me for a long time then, with an odd smile, she told me:

"Daddy is working more because you're going to be a big brother."

I nodded my head as if I understood.

"Oh," was all I said.

I didn't have a clue. I knew I was receiving important information, but I didn't know what it was. She patted her belly.

"Mommy is going to have a baby. Mommy is pregnant now. The baby is in Mommy's tummy right now, and in a few months the baby is going to come out and you'll be a big brother."

I looked at my mother in a whole new way. I had heard the words, but it was all too much to take in. The vision of one small human being living inside another was astonishing. *How could this happen? How does the baby eat while it's in there? How does it breathe? Does it have its eyes open? How does the baby get out? How do you know if it is a boy or a girl? Does Dad know about this?* These were mind-bending questions for an eight-year-old to deal with. I had to know one thing above all else. One question was way on the top of my list.

"How does the baby get inside?" I asked.

I watched my mother take a deep breath.

"Well," she said, "it starts with a seed. A seed grows inside you until the baby is big enough to be born. The baby is inside you for about nine months. Then it comes out of your stomach."

"Oh," I said again.

It seemed I had lost the ability to respond with any word other than "Oh." My mind was on fire with questions. *Seeds? What kind of seeds? How does the baby stay alive while it is inside you for nine months? How do you get the food to the baby? Can the baby throw up? If it does throw up, where does the puke go? Does it have hair? Does it sneeze? Does it break out of the belly like some kind of monster? How old is the baby when it comes out? Do different babies grow from different type of seeds? What happens when you go to the bathroom? What happens when IT goes to the bathroom? If you sneeze too hard, does the baby come out? If you eat two seeds, do you have twins?*

I was completely absorbed with these thoughts. I remember my legs leaving the table; about thirty seconds or so later my body followed behind. I followed my legs and caught up to them in my room. I was overwhelmed. For years I had been eating seeds without realizing the enormous risk I was taking. How was it that I was lucky enough not to have gotten pregnant? This was scary. Clearly I now had to avoid everything with seeds in it.

I started with the obvious—watermelon. It was difficult to begin with one of my favorites, but I had to be careful. Rye bread and cantaloupe were soon to follow. On November 22nd, Mom was making me some French toast. I got out the Mrs. Butterworth's syrup and was all set for my favorite breakfast. French toast was still okay with me, and I loved it. That was until I saw Mom get the eggs out of the refrigerator. I stared at the eggs. Even I knew eggs were chicken seeds.

" Mom, what are you doing with the eggs?"

"I need them for the French toast, honey."

"Wh . . . what?"

"I need them for the French toast. That's how you make French toast. First you put milk and eggs and sugar in a bowl and you mix—"

I grabbed my stomach.

"Are you all right?" she said. "What's the matter with your stomach?"

I was in agony. How could I have been so stupid! She was using eggs!! How could she have betrayed me? She was trying to ruin me. What else was she slipping eggs into?

"Why are you using eggs!" I screamed.

"What's wrong with you?"

"Why are you putting eggs in the French toast?"

The truth was it didn't matter. I realized I had to stay even more vigilant than before. Everything was suspect. Even though I couldn't stand them, cream cheese and butter were the only foods I really trusted. I dared not try the catsup (tomato seeds), or the mayo (I read about the deadly eggs on the label), and I secretly buried the A&P coffee bags in the backyard when Mom and Dad weren't looking. (I figured beans are seeds in disguise, and my parents were already in enough trouble.) But I was still confused about how come everyone wasn't pregnant. Does everybody in the world know what to avoid except me? I had seen people eat rye bread and watermelon and still not get pregnant. Is there an antidote you can take? Do you drink some anti-seed medication before enjoying a poppy-seed bagel? I was desperate to find the answers. I figured I would go to the number one authority on things to do with the body. I decided to talk to Ricky.

Ricky knew a lot about third grade because this was his third time in it. He was my best friend, but the truth was he was everybody's best friend. I am not really sure he even knew my name. He never called me by my name. He would say, "Hey, kiddo," or Hey, buuuuuuddy." He was older than me and knew a lot about how things in your body worked. He knew how to swallow air to make himself burp and how to make some very neat noises with his hand stuck in different parts of his body. He even knew how to make your finger feel numb and fold his eyelids back so they would look very gross—which was, of course, very cool. I knew he must know about the seeds. Anyone who knew how to make noises come from under his shirt had to know about the seed connection. I had seen Ricky eating grapes. I knew he was the one to ask. He had to know the antidote.

"Hey, Ricky!" I called to him in the cafeteria.

"Hey, kiddo!" he called back. We walked toward each other with our thumbs sticking straight up in the air. Ricky was cool. Very cool. Ricky knew how to blow one side of his nose at a time without a handkerchief. (In later years this would earn him the title of Snot-Rocket Master.) He could bend his thumb back so far he could touch his wrist. What a guy. I couldn't wait to ask him how he could afford to eat grapes. I knew it wasn't too cool to come right out and ask about the seeds. This was delicate politics. I needed the information, but I couldn't risk looking too stupid in front of Ricky. I was only eight and a half and Ricky was ten. He really had no reason to hang around with me at all, and if I were too much of a dimwit he would dump me. I figured I would eat lunch with him and let the topic come up naturally. We walked down the cafeteria line together. On my tray was the usual: eight butter patties, cream cheese on a plain bagel, milk, and an orange Creamsicle. To the untrained eye it was a typical eight-year-old's lunch; to the phobic gourmet it was another seed-free meal.

Ricky always brought his lunch from home. From his crumpled brown bag he unloaded the day's vicious little cargo. First was a pimento loaf-and-mustard sandwich on Wonder Bread; next he revealed a package of peanut M&M's; and safely tucked away at the bottom of the bag was a Granny Smith apple. Either Ricky knew the secret or this was his way of laughing in the face of death.

We sat across from each other and started eating. I watched in awe as Ricky opened up his pimento loaf sandwich and started sticking peanut M&M's strategically around it, a yellow one here, a red one there. He was fiendishly working on the seed machine. I could contain myself no longer.

"Ricky, what are you doing!?"

"My mom never lets me do this at home," he grinned.

"Well, of course not . . . no mom would let their kid do that to themselves . . ."

"Yeah. That's why I love to do it. You want some for your sandwich? Yours looks pretty plain."

"No!" I screamed. "I mean, no thanks. I mean, I don't know if I can stop it from happening if I eat one."

"What do you mean?"

"You know. Something starts out small . . . you know . . . and it gets larger . . . and larger . . . and . . . you know . . ."

"I know what you're talking about," he said as he chomped on the now crunchy sandwich, "but we don't have to worry about that kind of thing for another couple of years. My sister and brother—she's like fifteen and he is like seventeen or something like that—man, they worry about that stuff all the time. It's really gross. Isn't that the weirdest thing? Imagine worrying about what you eat because if you eat the wrong thing . . ." He shook his head and focused on a new color strategy for loading his M&M's into his sandwich.

"It's really gross and disgusting," I said, nodding in sincere agreement.

Ricky completed his sandwich preparation, nodded with satisfaction, then looked back up.

"Hey, have you ever seen what one looks like when it's almost ready to pop? I saw my brother in front of his mirror once. He was all freaked out because it was sticking out. I heard him say, 'Oh, shit!' Then he started squeezing it."

"You saw your brother squeezing it?" I said with my eyes popping out of my head.

"Yeah, it was disgusting. He squeezed it one way then another way for a while. I think he squeezed it so hard it finally popped."

I stopped breathing at this point. How could anyone be so crazy as to try and squeeze a baby out of his stomach? Ugh! Baby poops, blood, and belly guts. I was starting to get dizzy.

"Ricky, did you see what it looked like?"

"Oh, yeah," he said. "It had a big white head on it. I hear they all got either black heads or white heads, unless they're blind. I think that means that they don't have any head at all."

I lost it.

"What do you mean?" I said. "If the baby is blind, it still has a head, doesn't it? I mean, I understand that most babies would have white heads or black heads when they're born, but blind babies I am sure have heads. It's just, I think, their eyes don't work. I'm never eating another seed again! I never want to get pregnant! I'm eating cream cheese for the rest of my life!" I screamed.

Ricky didn't say much for a minute or two. He just sat there looking at me. I think he was trying to decide if he should get the school nurse or just make-believe he didn't know me.

"You think eating seeds can make you pregnant?" he asked.

I was committed. I had to tell him what I knew. I blurted it out. "Yeah."

Ricky squinted up his left eye and cheek as he shook his head. He fired off another question.

"What did you think I was talking about with my brother—a baby? Did you think he was trying to squeeze a *baby* out of his stomach? I was talking about a *pimple*. You get *pimples* if you eat the wrong food. You get *pimples*, not *pregnant*."

I was mortified. How did I get this so screwed up? I decided that the only way to save face was to confess to Ricky that I had no idea what I was talking about and ask him to tell me how someone gets pregnant.

"How does it happen, Rick? How does someone get pregnant?"

He started shaking his head up and down very slightly, and then spoke.

"I think I was about your age when I learned. It's pretty weird stuff. Are you sure you can handle it?"

"It can't be any weirder than thinking watermelon seeds make you pregnant."

Ricky laughed. Then he leaned across the table and began to whisper. "I can't tell you the details but I know what's involved . . ."

"What?" I whispered back.

Cupping his hand, Ricky whispered directly into my left ear. "Baby oil."

"Baby oil?" I said.

"Yeah, baby oil," he said, and wiggled his eyebrows.

"What about the baby oil?"

He stopped his eyebrows and turned them into a frown.

"That's *it*," he said. "*Baby oil* is where babies come from."

"Oh," I said. "Are you *sure* about that?"

"Positively," he said. "I heard it's even in the encyclopedia." Ricky grabbed my wrist and poured some of his M&M's into my hand. "Eat up, kiddo," he said. "There's no baby oil within a mile of this place."

I gobbled up the M&M's, free at last. That night I ate everything on my plate, and my parents chalked my aversion up to a "stage" I was going through. Everything was back to normal. I laughed thinking how stupid I had been to believe seeds could make me pregnant.

I even brought some of the coffee beans back in for Mom and Dad when I went out to bury the baby oil.

ᴄ

After I finished graduate school, to make extra money I signed up to administer psychological testing for the state. This type of testing was needed primarily for adults with what used to be called "mental retardation," people whose intellectual disability caused them to function at the cognitive level of a child. Because I had training as a developmental psychologist, I thought I could deal with this. I believed I had the skills, the talent, the patience, and the desire. I was limited by only one small fact, a minor detail missing from my repertoire of personal and professional experience: I had never actually met a person with an intellectual disability.

Enrico was a big man, very big. He was six feet four inches tall, and two hundred and forty-one pounds. He spoke broken English and had a measured IQ of fifty-two. His family was from Italy, and he had never had the opportunity to get any special education or training back in his country. Enrico's father was a wealthy businessman who shunned Enrico and only allowed him to work on their large estate. Enrico was an embarrassment. He was, however, used to doing lots of heavy physical labor. He was strong, but at the age of twenty-eight he knew nothing of the world. A simple, innocent man who knew only how to work hard.

His family moved to the United States for the business opportunities it afforded his father. The entire family—Enrico's mother and father, two sisters, four brothers, aunt, grandmother, housekeeper, gardener, and family dogs (there were six of them)—moved into a large home in the west end of our county. Within two weeks Enrico was lost and victimized in the new world. He had been arrested three times for exposing himself in public; he was beaten by a gang of youths who mistook him for a rival gang member; and he announced to his family that a woman named "Mary" would become his wife and have sex with him if he gave her a thousand dollars.

Welcome to America.

Somehow a local human-services agency got involved. No one was sure if the family made the referral, or if some well-meaning neighbor made the call but, in any case, the association realized what Enrico needed. He was quickly referred to the New Jersey Division of Developmental Disabilities (DDD). This is the official state office set up to provide services for people with intellectual disabilities. Because of his apparent

impairment and the lack of documentation from Italy, Enrico was identified as a person who needed psychological testing. I was both thrilled
and surprised when a social worker from the state called me to do the
testing. I had only recently submitted my name to their providers' list,
and I wondered why they would be calling me rather than a more experienced psychologist. When I questioned the social worker about this,
she gave me a simple two-word answer.

"You're new," she explained.

"Oh, I see, and I guess the state tries out new people to see if their
reports are any good."

"No."

"Just a random act of luck?"

"No. You're *new*."

"Yes, we've established that," I said trying to be funny. "I am new. But
how does this qualify me for the referral?"

"You said you would be willing to do testing for the state."

"Yes, I did."

"This means you are new."

"Just because I am willing to do testing for the state?"

"Yep. If you are willing to do testing for the state, you must be new."

"I guess established psychologists don't do much of this testing."

"That's right. Would you like to know how many psychologists there
are who are willing to do this kind of testing in this county?"

"Yes, I would."

"Two."

"Two?"

"Two."

"Wow," I said. "In the whole county there's only two. Who's the
other one?"

"Do you know Dr. Zimmer?"

"No, I'm afraid I don't."

"He's the other psychologist on the list."

"Is he new too?"

"Only psychologists at the beginning of their careers or at the end of their careers are willing to do this kind of testing."

"I guess he must be one of those psychologists at the end of his career."

"You might say that."

"I hate to be difficult about this, but that still leaves the question of why you chose me over him."

"He's dead."

"Dead?"

"Died two months ago."

"And he's still on the list?"

"Dr. Silverstein died in 1979, and he only got off the approved list last month."

The date was set for Enrico to come in. I decided to make the appointment for first thing in the morning. That way, if it took extra time I would be able to handle it. I wanted my first testing experience to be a good one. I wanted to leave plenty of time for problems, should they arise. My first paying customer for testing—I saw it as a privilege and a responsibility that I was the one to test Enrico to determine his eligibility for DDD services. I had tested many children and a few adults in graduate school, but I had never tested an adult with Enrico's rather unique problem. I was assured that Enrico was bilingual, and that testing him in English would be no problem. Right there I should have been suspicious. He was the one who is supposed to have the intellectual disability. My command of Italian was limited to "arrivederci."

I rented space in a building with a dozen or so other psychotherapists, including psychiatrists, and social workers, as well as psychologists. We had a common receptionist who attended to the patients for each of us. This was a building where you could go for a complete "checkup from the neck up." Each of the practitioners operated independently and, with the exception of myself, had well-established practices.

Enrico's size was imposing. When he walked into the waiting room I could see that the receptionist was a bit put off and nervous. A state social worker helped fill out the necessary paperwork. There was no doubt who my next patient was.

"How are you today, Enrico?" I said.

"I'm okay. Can I have a drink of water? I'm so thirsty."

I immediately went over to the water cooler and took a cup from the dispenser. When I handed him the water he said, "Thank you," and I felt we were off to a good start. He was polite, and I was accommodating. This should turn out well.

There were two kinds of tests the state wanted. One was a projective test. With this kind of test, a patient looks at an ambiguous image and gives meaning to it. When a person does this, it reveals what is on his or her mind. It can be considered a mental X-ray. The patient's responses give a clue to the psychologist about how the person's mind works. The second test was an IQ test to determine Enrico's intellectual ability. The projective tests were always more fun to do. You never knew what a person was going to say. I decided to start with the famous Rorschach "Inkblot" test—black-and-white pictures of ink droppings on an eight-by-ten-inch card.

The first image of the Rorschach test is the one most people have seen. It is the one where people often say they see a butterfly. I explained to Enrico that I was going to show him some pictures and that I wanted him to tell me what he saw when I showed them to him. He had some questions right away.

"Are dees your pictures?"

"Yes, they are, Enrico."

"You know what dey look like?"

"Yes, I do."

"If you know what dey look like, how come you gotta ask me?"

They never covered this in graduate school.

"They say you a doctor. Are you a doctor?"

"Yes . . . I'm a psychol—"

"Look at dis rash here."

Enrico stood straight up and started to unbuckle his pants.

"Dis rash here really hurts, but I no wanna show nobody because it's right dare."

I asked him to pull up his pants and told him I was the kind of doctor that just shows pictures and asks questions. He responded with a simple "Okay," and I decided to show him the first card.

"Enrico, I want you to take a look at this picture. Tell me what you see."

"Oh boy! Dis a picture of a women with no clothes on. She's gotta no clothes on right dare."

"Where do you see the woman with no clothes on?"

"Right dare. She gotta no clothes on, Doctor Dan."

I went on to the next card. With projective tests you look for a theme.

"Enrico, what do you see in this picture?"

"It's a different picture."

"What do you see in this picture?"

"Ah see *two* womens in the picture. Dey gotta no clothes. Right dare. No clothes. Ah love dem both. Ah want to have a baby with dem."

By the time I got to the third card I was nervous. Enrico saw a naked woman in the first card. On the second card he fell in love. What was waiting for us at card number three?

"Enrico?"

"Yeah."

"Enrico, I am going to show you this next card. Can I take the one you have up in front of your face?"

"Doctor Dan, Ah love dees womens. She dee mother of my child. Ah want to do . . . you know . . . make a baby with her."

"Enrico, I am going to take the card from you, and I want to show you this next card."

"Okay."

Enrico let me take the card from him. He dropped his head and murmured, "Ah love her, Ah love her." I immediately showed him the next card.

"Enrico, look at this card and tell me what you see."

I held the card up in front of him, and his eyes opened as wide as they possibly could. He was staring at two rather large blobs of black ink.

"Ohhhh, Doctor Dan, why you do dis to me? You make me feel bad when you show dis to me, Doctor Dan. Why you showing me dis?"

"Enrico, what do you see when you look at this picture?"

"You *know* what Ah see," he said.

"What is it, Enrico? What do you see?"

"It's another womens. She wants sex with me, but Ah no can do dat because Ah can't do dat. My family says Ah can't do dat with womens."

"Let me make sure I got this right. You see a woman in this picture that wants to have sex with you."

"Right."

"Can you show me where you see this woman?"

"Right dare."

"Right where? Can you point her out to me?"

"Right dare. Right dare!" He said getting excited. "She's right dare!!"

"Okay. Enrico. I just wanted to make sure I saw the same woman you did."

"She is right dare." He pointed to the inkblot. "You see her. She is right dare next to me!"

Enrico took the card in his hands and started kissing it. Here was a six foot four, 241-pound man French kissing an inkblot in my office at 8:30 in the morning.

I didn't need twenty years of schooling to figure out what was on Enrico's mind. What I did need was to have my own head examined. Why did I agree to do this in the first place? I decided to give up the projective testing (the theme had been established) and move right to the IQ test. Besides, I was only borrowing the Rorschach cards, and I wasn't sure they were saliva proof. Enrico was licking the cards as I tried to get his attention.

"Enrico?"

"MMMMMMmmmmmmOHHHHmmmmahh"

"Enrico?"

"MMMMMMM . . . wait, Doctor Dan, I'm not finished."

"Yes . . . well . . . I can see that . . . yes . . . you are not finished."

MMMMMMMMMMMMMMMmmmmmmmmmmmmmmmmm mmmmaahhhh . . ."

"Enrico. I really hate to do this—but I think some of the ink is actu-ally coming off the inkblot. I don't know much about these things, but I don't think that's a good thing."

"Am Ah doing the wrong ding, Doctor Dan?"

"No, Enrico, well not exactly, but I have another idea. I have some games I think you might like to play."

To my great surprise Enrico put the card down. It seemed like he liked games almost as much as he liked naked women hiding in inkblots.

"What games you got, Doctor Dan?"

"I have some games with blocks and puzzles and some symbols and some questions. Would you like to answer some fun questions?"

"Sure, Doctor Dan. Can Ah keep a picture of my womens?"

"Actually, Enrico, the picture doesn't belong to us. It belongs to someone else."

"The womens belong to someone else?"

"Yes . . . in a way they do."

"Den I can no touch the womens. Dey belong to someone else."

I'm not sure if I was relieved or just surprised. Enrico handed me the saliva-soaked card and spoke:

"Tell the man with the womens dey are beautiful womens and Ah never touch dem no more."

"I'll tell him, Enrico. Will you do me a favor and answer some ques-tions for me?"

"Sure. Ah can do it."

"Good."

"Do dey got to be right?"

"Your answers?"

"Yeah, I'm good at answering questions if dey don't got to be right."

"You just give it your best shot."

"Doctor Dan, somebody got a gun?"

"No, no. 'Give it your best shot' means 'try your best.'"

"Uh-huh. Try my best what?"

"Best answer."

"Okay. You got any more questions?"

"We haven't started yet, Enrico. I'm going to ask you a question in a few minutes."

"That's okay. Take your time."

"Enrico, what are the colors of the American flag?"

"Which one?"

"Which one?"

"Which American flag? In North America dey got flags different than the flags in South America. Which flag you mean?"

Did I have a savant on my hands? I had read about these incredible people who had extremely low IQs, but were absolutely brilliant in some obscure area. Could it be that Enrico was intellectually disabled, but some kind of geography expert?

"Enrico, I want to know the color of the flag of the United States of America. Do you know that one?"

"No, Ah don't know no flags."

"How about from other countries?"

"No. WAIT! Ah think one of dem is yellow—no, orange. It's a good flag."

So much for my theory on Enrico-the-Savant. I pressed on.

"Enrico, why do we put stamps on letters?"

"'Cause my momma hits me if Ah put them on my mirror."

"Yes, well, okay. Where should we put them?"

"Not on mirrors."

"Right. Good. Not on the mirrors. Very good. But where should we put them?"

"Ah don't think dey go on mirrors."

"No, I don't think so either. Where do you think the stamps should go?"

"On the mirrors. Dey look great on dare."

"Okay, how about the next question?"

"Okay."

"Enrico, can you tell me how an orange and a banana are alike?"

"Oh, dat's a tough one. Let's see, an orange and a banana. Dat's a tough one. Ah know! Dey both like the moon at different times."

"What was that, Enrico?"

"Dey both like the moon at different times. Dat was a tough one. You got more?"

"Are there any other ways an orange and a banana are alike?"

"No, dat's it."

"Enrico, can you name two things that are round?"

"Sure," he said as he smiled and opened his eyes wide.

"Can you say them out loud?"

"It's okay for me to say out loud?"

"Sure it is. Go ahead. Tell me two things that are round."

"Boobs."

Enrico held his hands in front of his chest as if he were holding two enormous breasts. I started laughing, and this made Enrico laugh.

"Dat's the right answer, eh, Doctor Dan. Ah can tell dat's the right answer 'cause you know that too, right? Womens got two tings dat are round right here," he said as he gestured with his hands in front of his own chest again. "Dat's the right answer. You ever see dem, Doctor Dan? You ever see women's breasts?"

I was still laughing. I remember covering a lot of things in my testing course, but somehow this topic never was part of the curriculum.

"You're too much, Doctor Dan. How come you asking me dees silly questions? What dey for? First you show me naked womens, then you ask about the soft cover books with more pictures of naked womens, and now you laughing about women's boobs. You a funny guy."

I stopped laughing and spoke to Enrico.

"Good point. What are these tests for? Good point. Well, these tests will help the State of New Jersey, hopefully, give you some money for training and programs and stuff like that."

"Dat's what my father said. He was right. My father said dat's why we come to New Jersey."

"I don't understand, Enrico. Why did you come to New Jersey?"

"My father says New Jersey gots money. Streets are made with money, but Ah don't see money in the streets. Dat's what Ah was looking for when Ah got beat up by dose boys. Ah was looking in the streets for money in New Jersey, but no luck."

"I understand. But it really isn't that way, Enrico. The state will pay for you to go to a program to help you learn how to get a job. They won't actually hand you money. It's like you'll be going to school."

"Ah never went to school, Doctor Dan. My father says Ah can never go to school. It's no good for me to go."

"How come it's not good for you to go to school?"

"Ah got, Ah got, Ah got . . . a bad head. My father said to me."

It was the first time I had heard Enrico stutter.

"He, he, he, he tells me all the time Ah got no good head for school. He says my brain is no good. It's no good, he says. My brain is no good."

"Do you believe that, Enrico?"

"Ah don't want to go to school, Doctor Dan. My father says dey gonna laugh if Ah go to school. Ah don't want to go. Ah just get the womens and has the babies with her. Hey," he said suddenly wide-eyed and excited, ". . . let's take some more tests. Ah like dees tests, Doctor Dan. Hey, how my doing with the tests? You think New Jersey gonna say Ah pass my tests?"

"Enrico," I said earnestly, "I think New Jersey is going to be very, very good to you."

"Ah love New Jersey."

I finished the testing and wrote up the report. I recommended a pre-vocational training program that would eventually help Enrico get a job while also developing some social skills. As a long-range goal I asked that the Division of Developmental Disabilities accept Enrico into their system for future residential placement in a group home. I also requested he have therapy to help him deal with social and interpersonal skills. To be specific I asked the state to consider putting him in group psychotherapy.

Within two weeks of testing Enrico, I had seven new referrals for testing. I had become the only living psychologist on the approved list.

I lost track of Enrico and immersed myself in doing testing for the state. While not everyone had the problems Enrico had, each person with an intellectual disability who came through the door had a unique view of the world and, along with that, a unique group of problems to deal with. In nearly every situation I recommended therapy as a way to help him or her cope with life.

What I didn't realize was that no one *did* therapy for people with intellectual disabilities—no one.

It was the spring of 1983, and I was thrilled to have more and more testing to do. By the time summer came around I had one full day a week devoted to testing. By the end of the summer, two full days had been set aside. I dedicated myself to building up my practice and securing a teaching position. It wasn't until November of 1985 that I got another call from Joann, the state social worker who originally told me why I had been picked to do the testing. She was usually the one to call to set up a testing appointment, but this call was different.

"Hi, Dan, do you remember Enrico?"

"How could I forget him?"

"I need your help with him."

"He doesn't need a follow-up test already, does he?"

"No, he doesn't need more testing. What he needs is a therapist."

"You mean they are only getting around to my recommendation for therapy now?"

"Nobody *does* therapy for these people."

"What do you mean? I know quite a few mental health clinics in the county."

"They don't want to work with them. They're afraid. Everybody has the same excuse. 'No one on our staff has had any training in how to work with people who are retarded. We can't help you.'"

"Can they really say that?"

"They do. Besides, the few times that we have pushed the clinics to take one of our people, they drop them after two or three sessions. They really don't want to do it."

"You want me to see Enrico for therapy?"

"You're the only one I can think of who would at least give him a chance."

"I hate to say this, but the truth is I never had any training in how to *do* therapy with someone like Enrico."

"Do you think *anyone* has been trained to treat him?"

"Good point."

"If you're interested, you can call the agency. He is living there now in a group home. He moved in two months ago, and things have been pretty wild. They can fill you in on the details. If you are willing to do this, we will pay you through the agency. There is money set aside for this kind of consultation."

"Joann, thanks for thinking of me with this."

"Hey, who else do I know on the 'approved' list?"

"Right. I'll call the agency and see what they say."

This particular agency ran group homes, vocational programs, and prevocational programs for people with IQs below 70. I called and told them I was the psychologist the state had recommended to work with Enrico. The woman on the other end of the phone let go a litany of complaints about him. In the brief two months he had been in the home, Enrico had managed to bite off a piece of his "girlfriend's" ear; to crack the shinbone of a staff member who had told him to strip his bed and wash the sheets; to rip the earring out of the ear of a woman who walked through his group home on a job interview; to knock a male staff member unconscious because he was standing too close to him; and to bite through the tongue of a woman he was kissing. In case all the bodily harm he had caused was not enough, he had laid waste to his room by punching holes in the walls and breaking each of the windows three times.

What amazed me about this list of volatility was that I never would have predicted it. Sure, Enrico was big and his view of the world was distorted, but I didn't think for a minute that he was the kind of person who was out to do harm. Before coming to the United States, he had no history of anything violent. What was going on here?

I decided that since all of Enrico's aggression took place in his group home, I should visit him there rather than have him come to the office. Somehow this just made sense to me. But the group home manager for the agency was shocked and a bit disoriented when she found out I wanted to come to the house.

"You want to interview Enrico at the house?"

"Will that be all right?"

"You're a psychologist and you want to interview Enrico here, not at your office?"

"If that's okay."

"We have never had a psychologist come to the house."

"Well, I have never been to a group home, so we're even."

"Oh, wow, I can't believe you're coming here."

"It sounds like maybe you'd rather I not come."

"See, that's the kind of thing that scares me. You could figure what was going on in my mind when I never even said it. How did you do that? Are you going to analyze us? Like, do you know what I'm thinking and stuff? I don't know if I can handle it."

People often get weird around psychologists. But this staff person seemed to have a weirdness all her own. I tried not to be too serious about it.

"Yes, I understand. But the truth is I'm just coming to see Enrico."

"So, you won't analyze the staff?"

"See, you figured that out and I didn't even say it."

"Oh, wow, so maybe like I'm psychic or something. Do you study that stuff? Like, is there a test or something that you could give me that would determine if I'm psychic?"

"I knew you were going to ask me that."

"Oh, wow, that's very cool. How did you do that?"

"I was only kidding."

"Oh, wow. Sure, I bet they teach you to say that—but you really knew. That's cool. Wow."

"Can I come see Enrico around seven o'clock Thursday night?"

"Wow, this Thursday?"

"It's amazing how you knew that. Of all the Thursdays there are going to be, you knew it would be this Thursday."

"This Thursday's cool. What time?"

"I bet you even know that."

"Seven o'clock?"

"Incredible."

"Wow. Cool. Okay. Seven o'clock this Thursday."

I hung up the phone and marked down the appointment in my calendar. On Thursday evening I drove out to Enrico's group home and was surprised to find a beautiful, large ranch house with a manicured lawn. Twelve residents lived there, six men and six women. Enrico was the twelfth to move in, and the most problematic. I knocked on the door and a young woman with Down syndrome answered.

"Hello, I'm Dr. Tomasulo. I came here to see Enrico."

"I'm Judy."

"Hello, Judy."

"You want Enrico?"

"Yes, I'm here to see him."

"Okay."

Judy shut the door, and that was that. I waited for about two minutes and knocked on the door again. Judy opened it.

"Hello, I'm Dr. Tomas—"

"You again!"

"Judy, I'm here to see Enrico."

"I know that."

"Can I see him?"

"He's in his room."

"Can I come in?"

"I can't let strangers into the house."

"Good, right. You did the right thing. Of course, I am a stranger, and you did the right thing. Is there a staff person I could talk to?"

"Do you want to speak to Susan?"

"Yes."

"She's not here today."

"Is there someone else working today?"

"Yes, there is."

"Who is working today?"

"Amy."

"Can I speak with Amy?"

"I'll get her."

Judy shut the door again. This time a different woman opened the door.

"Hello, I'm Dr. Tomasulo"

"You're the psychologist?"

"Yes. I'm here to see Enrico."

"We had it on the schedule that you were going to be here seven o'clock this morning."

"No, no. It was 7 p.m. I was going to be here."

"Oh, well, we had 7 a.m. marked down in the book."

"Is it okay to see Enrico now?"

"I guess so. Come on in."

Inside the house was spacious and very pleasant—nothing fancy, but everything was very clean. It was hard to believe that twelve people lived there with a minimum of two staff on every shift. It was a *very* nice home.

Amy showed me to Enrico's room and warned me that Enrico didn't like to be disturbed. She said a lot of the problems that had happened took place when Enrico was disturbed. She left me alone in front of his door. With some trepidation I knocked twice. Enrico was quick to respond.

"Go away. Ah don't wants to be bothered."

"Enrico, it's Doctor Dan. I came to see you."

Enrico pulled open his door. In the three years since I'd seen him he had gained forty pounds. He had on glasses and a pair of boxer shorts covered by a long flannel shirt. Enrico was thrilled to see me.

"Hey, Doctor Dan, it's a long time that Ah see you. You going to show me the pictures with the naked womens again? Ah no see dem for a long time. Ah like you, Doctor Dan. Let's see the pictures."

"Can I come into your room?"

"Sure, dat's fine with me."

He gave me a big handshake and invited me into his room. I asked him to show me around, and he obliged. It was like being taken on a tour of the bedroom of a sixteen-year-old boy whose parents hadn't been in his room for a long, long time.

Enrico immediately went to the *Playboy* magazines he had under his mattress. They were worn and ripped and had Enrico's trademark saliva stains all over them. He had magazine pictures of cars all over the room. Each of the cars had a woman hanging on it, and it was hard to tell if Enrico had any interest in cars or if they simply made a good backdrop for his real fascination. I had learned that the staff so feared Enrico that no one set foot in his room—ever. This was against the agency's policies, but if Enrico even thought anyone had gone into his room he would rage against the whole house. People in the house were afraid. I wasn't sure I could help.

His bed looked as if it hadn't been made in weeks. The room had a distinctive and unpleasant odor to it, which seemed to be coming from the bed. It smelled like old urine and maybe vanilla. I sat on the corner of the bed and asked Enrico some questions.

"Enrico, some people asked me to come here and talk with you because of the problems you're having. Is it okay if we talk about that?"

"Dat's okay, Doctor Dan. We can talks about it."

"Can you tell me what made you so angry, Enrico? It seems like something must have made you upset."

"Stuff makes me so much pain, Doctor Dan. Ah can't do it no more. Den Ah hit somebody 'cause Ah hurts so much."

"Enrico, I'm sorry, I don't understand. What's the stuff that causes you so much pain that you have to hit somebody?"

"The sex thing dat makes it hard, Doctor Dan. It gets hard, den I got blood. I can't stand when pain is down dare."

"Blood?"

"Blood down dare, Doctor Dan. Dat white stuff no come out no more."

"Enrico, I don't really understand what you mean. Where are you bleeding?"

In one move Enrico reached past me and grabbed the opposite corner of the bedcovers and pulled them back. In the middle of the sheets were half-dried blotches of blood and sperm. Hundreds of splattered bits of Enrico had become the permanent color of his sheets. The dark reds and yellows revealed the deeper source of the odor in the room. There were dozens of pictures from the *Playboys* all crumpled and stained with the same colors that were on the sheets. Enrico pointed to the secret he had been concealing.

"Pain is there. Ah bleeds every day down there, Doctor Dan."

I spent over an hour with Enrico talking about his pain. What I found out was that Enrico didn't know how to masturbate. He had never learned about lubrication and would pull on himself every night until he bled. As best I could tell from his description, he would try to ejaculate before he felt so much pain from the bleeding that he had to stop. I told him I would help him and made arrangements to see him the following night. As I left him I asked him if he would do me a favor.

"Enrico, would you do me a favor just for tonight?"

"Sure, Doctor Dan. Ah like talking to you. Ah feel better."

"Well, good, Enrico, I feel better too. Will you do me one favor for tonight?"

"Favor for you? Ah do it."

"Give it a rest."

Enrico looked at me for the longest time. I remembered reading that some people with an intellectual disability need eighteen seconds to process information. I could see that Enrico needed every last one of these seconds for this request to get through. Finally he started a slow broad grin that worked itself into a full out-and-out belly laugh. He was laughing as hard as ever when he spoke.

"Ahhhhhhhhhhh, Doctor Dan, you a funny guy. Give it rest. Dat's good. Ah no touch it tonight, Doctor Dan. Ah give it a rest."

I gave Enrico a high five and opened up his bedroom door. He was laughing and shaking his head as I walked out. I kept hearing him repeat himself.

"Dat Doctor Dan's a funny guy; 'give it a rest.' Tonight, Ah give it a rest."

The next night I was there at seven o'clock sharp, and Enrico greeted me at the door. He looked as if he had just downed thirty cups of espresso. To say the least, he was eager to talk.

"Ah gave it a rest, Ah gave it a rest, Ah gave it a rest, Doctor Dan. Ah no touch mahself all night."

Enrico was talking very loud and very fast, and there were at least a half dozen others in the house who could hear him. I told him he had done the right thing and asked if we could talk in his room. When we got there, his bed had been made and his room straightened. He seemed delighted and told me he washed everything and even cleaned his closet. I was surprised yet troubled by such dramatic changes. If Enrico kept his hands off himself for a few more days, he'd be tidying up the State of New Jersey.

I had friends in the field of special education who provided me with commercially produced line drawings used for sex education. The line drawings were to educate rather than stimulate. They were clearly designed to be instructive, not erotic. Enrico was already rubbing his crotch.

"Hey, great, Doctor Dan, you bring more pictures for me to look at. Ah like pictures you show me. We got naked womens, Doctor Dan?"

I sat with Enrico for two hours and showed him pictures and answered his questions. He listened intently and every once in a while made a noise such as, "OHHHHHHHhhhhhh." On occasion he would mumble some words, "Dat's how dat works," or some such utterance. He was completely absorbed in his education. Finally, it came time to teach about lubrication.

"Enrico, when your penis gets like in the picture, you have to put some kind of lubrication on, something to make your hand go smoother. Do you understand what I am saying?"

"Smoother, right?"

"Right. You can use anything that makes it go smoother. Do you know what Vaseline is?"

"We got some. Ah don't use it for smoother."

"Yes, you put a little bit of it on your hand and that will keep you from hurting. Why don't you go get some and keep it by your bed, and when your penis gets like this in the picture, use it so you won't bleed. Okay?"

"Okay. Ah get it now."

Enrico was gone for a longer time than I expected. As I sat writing notes in his room I could hear his distinctive, lumbering footsteps plodding down the hall. I also heard the faint sloshing of a liquid that seemed to keep pace with his bulky footsteps. My back was to him and, as he came to the doorway, a whiff of petroleum seemed to have arrived with him. I turned around to see Enrico holding a bright red round can of gasoline with yellow lettering and a white nozzle. He had already put some on his right hand.

"No no no no no no no no noooooooooooooo . . . not *gasoline*! *Vaseline*!" I screamed.

Immediately I had visions of headlines in the *Daily News*: SHRINK BLOWS PATIENT UP DURING SEX LESSON. I had to fix this fast. I told Enrico to wash his hands while I put the gasoline can back in the group home's garage. I washed my hands and went back to his room to talk.

"Enrico, maybe we shouldn't use *Vaseline*. Maybe we should use baby oil. Do you have baby oil?"

Enrico's face changed instantly. He looked worried and began to frown. He grabbed the line drawings I left on his desk and went to the one where the woman is pregnant. Enrico pointed to it as he spoke.

"No, Doctor Dan, Ah can't use baby oil. Baby oil makes *BABIES!* Dat's how dey do it, Doctor Dan. Baby oil makes babies."

Even though I had heard him perfectly well, I asked him to repeat it.

"What did you say?" I asked.

"Baby oil, Doctor Dan, baby oil makes babies!"

I am in the lunchroom with Ricky. He is putting M&M's on his sandwich and telling me how his brother squeezes pimples.

"Sit back down, Enrico," I say. "We have to talk."

Enrico sits and looks at me expectantly.

"Enrico," I begin, "We need to talk." I paused, struggling to choose my words carefully. "Well, it starts with a seed . . ."

Kettle of Fish

On the back of his right hand the roots of a marijuana plant are growing between his fingers. The tattoo spreads over his knuckles, following his veins, until disappearing under the cuff of his blue-and-white-striped Van Heusen. The purple stem and distinctive pointy green leaves scramble up under the sleeve and emerge above his collar. The leaves and stems cross under his neck and disappear into the other side of his shirt. On the back of his left hand, the intense purple-and-green plant is so lush no natural flesh tone is visible. The dark blue suit he wears provides an unlikely background for such a mural. The tattoo is ten years old, a memento of his eighteenth birthday. The suit is new, chosen by the mortician this morning.

Gary grew up on MacDougal Street in New York's Greenwich Village with his alcoholic parents. Since he was my second cousin, we spent lots of time together when we were kids. Sundays his family and mine would eat dinner at my grandparents' on West Fourth Street. In the summer, Sunday dinner moved to my grandparents' cottage in Edgewater, New

Jersey. Here the grown-ups would sit, eat, laugh, smoke, and drink in the screened-in porch, while Gary and I disappeared into our transgressions.

On a hill in a red wagon two four-year-old boys prepare their flying carpet. Gary sits in front holding on to the black handle. I'm sitting behind with my legs wrapped around him. We start to roll. He's steering, and I'm pushing with asphalt-blackened hands. We've done this before. The paved road is steep and skinny with turns, and the big black handle is too much for him to control. We hit a rock. The wagon tips over, spilling us screaming into the street. Cuts on our legs, hands, and elbows. We practice cursing. There is blood, and we compare scrapes and mutilations. We right the wagon. It is my turn to pull it up the hill. The nearly deserted road becomes our personal slalom for longer, faster, and more dangerous rides. Each attempt has one ultimate goal: not to crash. We are never successful, yet the afternoon is pure pleasure. We spend it screaming, crashing, and laughing. By dark we are hungry and make our way back to the cottage. There are gasps when we walk in.

"What the hell happened to you?"

"Oh my God, you're both bleeding!"

"Are you all right?"

"Who did this to you?"

"Were you two fighting?"

"Look at what you did to your shirt!"

Gary's mother says nothing. She is unconscious, decorating the run-down couch on the porch. Overweight and unattractive, she is curled, fetal-style, on the black plastic cushions. Her curly, dark brown hair is straw dry; her face and eyeballs yellow from her deteriorating liver. Even though I'm just a kid, I realize there is something wrong. Around her eyes the skin is gray and doughy. If you could stand to look at her, you would notice the large, blood-rich veins in each of her eyes. She smells of Scotch and Romano cheese.

Her name is Enis. (Gary was embarrassed because it rhymed with penis.) Mickey is Gary's father: short, round, and balding. Despite what friends and relatives advise, Mickey rakes strands of thin hair across his gleaming bald head. Tonight it looks particularly bad. He is drunk and his eyes seem permanently hollow and black. Gary and I watch as he stumbles and yells. This is my first recollection of his family.

During high school Gary worked in a bar called the Kettle of Fish directly below his parents' apartment. He cleaned up, waited on tables, and ran errands for the owner. The bar wasn't more than a thousand square feet. As you walked in, you were in the far right corner of the establishment. To the left, along the entire length of the wall, was a huge mahogany-trimmed mirror. Except for a small rounded section near the large front window, the well-worn wooden bar ran the complete length. Four booths sat along the right wall with wooden church -pew-style seats capable of holding three people on each side. A dozen wooden stools with imitation black leather tops hugged the brass foot rail along the bottom of the bar. The top was wider than most bars and had been shellacked more times than anyone could remember. A mahogany lip matching the mirror capped the long edge of the bar. Behind the bar in front of the mirror a standard offering of liquors stood waiting. Only two beers on tap: Guinness and Budweiser. The sidewalls were the original brick of the building, and the old, odd-sized floorboards were covered in sawdust and peanut shells. At any given time it was three people deep at the bar, and the booths were jammed. The place had a strong lunch trade and was packed every night with both locals and tourists. Except for the door, the rest of the front of the bar was a window etched with a calligraphy sign in arched letters reading "Kettle of Fish." Other than its location, it is hard to determine the attraction. The booze was cheap and the food good, but that was true for a half dozen bars along MacDougal. None of them had the business traffic of the Kettle. Everybody came through there: sailors, actors, Mafiosi, writers, homeless people, druggies, street comics, and the wandering insane. Everybody and anybody came there. By the time he graduated from high school, Gary knew them all.

On a typical day Gary would come home from high school, drink red wine with his mother until she fell asleep, and then go downstairs to work in the Kettle. Some days he'd skip school, and he and his mother would start drinking as soon as they got up—around noon. When

I was a senior I had a legitimate day off from school and went into the city to visit my grandmother. I went to Gary's place first to see if he was home. At about two in the afternoon, he and Enis were already midway through a half-gallon of wine. I had entered a foreign country. At seventeen, staying home and getting drunk with your mother was something I couldn't begin to imagine. It was hard enough to be around my mother when she was stone-cold sober. Polishing off a bottle of wine together was out of the question. My uncle drove a truck delivering religious articles for the Archdiocese of New York. Once he made his deliveries he was free to leave. On this particular day he arrived home about twenty minutes after I had gotten there, and we all sat down and finished the wine. What planet was I on?

⌒

Fragments of memories and conversations hover like aircraft waiting for clearance to land. I am still in shock from the phone call from another cousin telling me he is dead. The details were sketchy, but the fact is that he died sometime after 4 a.m. At the funeral I half expected him to sit up in the coffin. It seems crazy now, but I remembered a time when I was jealous of him. Gary was offered a full scholarship to NYU to study filmmaking. I was as happy for him as I was envious. He never seemed to study, drank almost every day, and wouldn't have to pay for his education. My parents had made no other provision for me to go to school; I was paying for it myself. One day while I was home on break from college, I went into New York and stopped in the Kettle to see if Gary was there. By then, I hadn't seen him in about three years.

He was taller and much thinner than I remembered him: nearly six feet and not more than 150 pounds. He had a beard and a ponytail. He stood behind the bar wearing an undershirt and washing out a beer mug. A cigarette was fixed in the corner of his mouth. An elaborate tattoo in the design of a marijuana plant was etched up his right arm across his neck and down his left. It was both grotesque and startling. I came in, he looked up and in one move jumped over the bar. He was hugging and introducing me to anyone who would listen. He smelled terrible.

He told me how he dropped out of school his first semester to manage the Kettle. In one long sentence he explained that he didn't drink so much now since he'd found pot, cocaine, and heroin. I heard him say heroin and tried not to betray the shock I felt. He rattled off a list of actors, comics, and musicians he's shot up with. Tales of insane drug parties with the likes of John Belushi and James Taylor followed. Gary saw me staring at the tattoo and explained. It covered his track marks. The purple stems of the plant followed his veins everywhere he shot dope. His friends showed similar, though more subdued versions. I was scared for him. I didn't know who he was. In two hours he introduced me to thirty people, all of them junkies.

⌇

At the funeral I'm staring at his dark blue suit and matching tie and realizing that only hours ago we were partying together. We had renewed our connection. After seeing Gary for the first time as a junkie in April of 1972, I didn't see him again until October of 1976. That was when I started graduate school in New York and hung out with him every Thursday night. By then his mother, Enis, had died and his father, my uncle Mickey, had moved out, leaving Gary the apartment. He had been through half a dozen rehab programs and had managed to become a "chipper," someone who doesn't mainline all the time, but "chips" his skin with the needle to get the heroin into his system. Because chipping is subcutaneous, it is considered less of a threat. On Thursdays I had class at six in the evening. After class I walked from Fifth and Thirteenth down to the Kettle and hung out at the bar until it closed at 2 a.m. I'm amazed at the range of people he knew: cops, bums, big-time actors, small-time crooks, street comics, and even a few musclemen from both the Irish Mafia (the Murphia, he called them) and their local competitors, the Sons of Italy. I'd be lying if I said it wasn't fun. For me, the array of people streaming into the bar was half an education; watching Gary deal with them was the other half.

One night eight sailors from New Zealand come into the bar looking for trouble. They are already drunk and think they are hot shit. They don't know that there are at least fifteen people in the bar, including Gary, who have guns and need very little provocation to take them out or to use them. They are dressed in white sailor uniforms, and I see the nastiest one of them cooking up a plot to start a fight. In a moment the plan is put into play. The guy orders a cheeseburger, beer, and fries. Gary gives him the beer, and when the burger is done, places it with the fries on a paper plate. The guy puts a ten-dollar bill on the bar, and Gary gives him change. Then it starts. The sailor has watched Gary drink all night and figures he's looped. He starts screaming that he gave Gary a twenty and only got back change for a ten. They swap insults. The guy raises his voice and starts cursing at Gary. "You fucking long-haired douche bag. What kind of fucking faggot are you with a tattoo all over your body? Give me change for my twenty, you asshole, or I'll wipe the floor with you!" There is instant tension in the room, but Gary is calm, smiling, and to the fifteen folks who would love to end the dispute right then and there, Gary gently closes his eyes and gives a slight shake of his head. He is taking care of this.

He reaches under the bar, takes out a bat, and slams it down on the hamburger. The meat, cheese, and fries splatter right onto the sailor's chest. Gary sticks the bat in the guy's face. "I'm pretty fucking sure you gave me a ten. Now you've got two choices: you and your asshole buddies buy everybody in this fucking bar a drink, or get the fuck out of here right now." The eight of them turn the color of wet toilet paper. The guy who instigated the whole thing raises his mug in the air: "Drinks all around!" he yells. The bar cheers and by the end of the night the eight sailors are everyone's friends. The Kettle closes with them teaching us their national anthem.

In his last year, Gary was in a methadone-maintenance program where the physician gave him double his dosage. Gary would sell it on the street and buy himself heroin. The money from the sale of the second dose went back to the physician. Apparently, this wasn't unusual. Gary told me of other junkies who did the same thing at other centers around the city. The truth was, Gary was actually doing less dope, but it still had a hold on him. I asked him once what it was like to have this addiction.

"Remember when we were kids and would try to hold the beach ball under the water at the pool at Palisades Amusement Park?" he asked.

"Sure."

"Remember, we would time it and try to keep it down as long as we could?"

I nodded, not yet understanding his point.

"That's what an addiction is," he said. "You hold it down for as long as you can, but at some point you're gonna slip, and it's gonna come screaming up and get away from you."

The month before I started graduate school Gary's girlfriend had moved in with him.

"Kristine's a whore and a junkie," he told me. "She never wears a bra or panties—says it slows her down. She's what I call a sexual savant."

He was somehow proud of this. He told me he never minded what she did on her own time, as long as she came home to him. Her blazing red hair went just beyond her shoulders and rested on the top of her breasts. Her lime green eyes could penetrate and stimulate. Her favorite color was red, and it was rare not to see her wearing it. Sensuality dripped from her; she flirted with men just to stay in practice. Despite her addiction, her body was remarkably appealing. She hadn't yet lost the smooth firmness of the flesh as most female junkies do.

It was Kristine who found Gary. He was lying on the couch with the needle still sticking out of a purple stem in his left arm. The story went that after the bar had closed and I left, Gary went back to his apartment with a friend named Jake who was raving about the new dope he had. Gary and Jake shot up together. Because Gary was chipping, he hadn't built up the kind of tolerance needed to withstand strong heroin. When Kristine came home about 4:30 in the morning she tried to wake them. Jake got up and realized what happened. He left, and Kristine called the police.

The funeral had a surreal quality to it. It seemed as if one representative from every walk of life showed up. Somehow Mickey, Kristine, and I were together in the limo behind the hearse. They were both roaring drunk and had been for the three days during the wake. Kristine carried a pint of Southern Comfort in her purse while Mickey carried a half-pint of Dewar's in his inside jacket pocket. They made no attempt to hide it. Even the people at the funeral parlor on Bleecker Street asked them to be more discreet. Preferring to bask in the ultimate excuse for obliteration, they ignored these requests.

Kristine attached herself to my uncle's side from the moment Gary was laid out. By the time of the funeral they were inseparable. They were clutching and drinking like they were on a first date, and crying together as if they were husband and wife. In the limo out to Long Island, Kristine sat in the middle between Mickey and me. Barely acknowledging me, they drank and cried. Their self-absorbed grief gave way to kissing while Kristine ran her left hand across Mickey's crotch, and Mickey discovered Kristine wore no panties. I was sickened, startled, aroused, saddened, and disgusted. Usually whenever I feel too much of anything I start to laugh, but this time I went numb.

At the grave the priest said something about Gary not having the opportunity to yet make his mark, and Mickey mumbled, "He made his mark all up and down his arm." The remark was a trigger for his rage, and with Kristine holding on to his right arm, Mickey threw his Dewar's bottle with his left arm toward Gary's blank headstone.

The small bottle tumbled end over end with a few drops of Scotch spiraling out of its top. The throw put Mickey off balance, and he jabbed his right leg out in front of him for support. Kristine tried to pull him back, but she was too weak and let out a soft, sloppy giggle. She covered her face with her free hand and yanked harder, pulling Mickey away from the mouth of the grave. The spray from the bottle made a thin line of Scotch on the coffin, and when it shattered against the blank headstone, you could hear a muffled "pop," like a small-caliber gun going off in the distance.

⌒

I liked Steve right from the start. He was a practicing Buddhist, intelligent and thoughtful. His serenity radiated through the room. He was centered, well read, and conversant on a wide variety of topics. He could talk about timing on a Mercedes 190 SL as easily as he could extol the virtues of a Martin D12-D28, 1935 Starburst guitar. Before becoming a Wall Street broker he had been a studio guitarist for years. His name appeared on dozens of major rock albums. He had photos of himself playing with Led Zeppelin, but his greatest memory was jamming with Eric Clapton and the progressive rock group Blind Faith when they toured Helsinki in 1969. Hands down, he thought, they were the greatest rock group of all time.

Steve had been busted two years before I met him when he was shooting five-thousand-dollars' worth of heroin a day. On Wall Street he had been a major supplier of both heroin and cocaine. He was busted by federal narcotics agents for selling two hundred and fifty thousand dollars of heroin and cocaine a week and then he was hospitalized to help him through the withdrawal. As part of the plea bargain, the conditions of his release included individual therapy. He was still on an ankle bracelet from the drug-rehabilitation program when he first came to my office. Steve was my patient.

As soon as he went into the rehab program he joined both Alcoholics Anonymous and Narcotics Anonymous. When you start these 12-step programs the typical advice is to make 90 meetings in 90 days. Steve did this—for both. He attended 180 meetings in 90 days.

That was Steve. It was clear, as our sessions continued, that Steve never did anything half assed. He always gave himself over to whatever he was doing. It didn't matter if it was learning about antique Mercedes, practicing a new riff on the guitar, or shooting heroin; Steve would do it perfectly, obsessively, until he was bored with it. Once he started working on Wall Street, he *never* played a guitar in a studio again. When the Mercedes became old hat, he gave it away to his niece. Once he finished with something, that was it. By the age of thirty-eight Steve had had dozens of girlfriends but, not surprisingly, he had never married.

His heroin habit exploded once he started on Wall Street. He told me stories of seven-hundred-dollar lunches for two people in which the fine wine billed to his American Express card was actually a five-hundred-dollar bag of cocaine supplied by the waiter. The 2 p.m. demand for drugs on the floor of the exchange (the beginning of what Steve called the *real* rush hour—everyone's second hit of the day) was, according to Steve, "so great that if you had enough product you could make a thousand dollars a minute between 2 and 3 p.m." He had connections with the Mob, contacts in Chinatown, and "friends" in Harlem. To support his heroin habit, he skimmed from everyone. "I was an equal-opportunity junkie," he said. "It didn't matter who I ripped off." He had been lucky and had never ripped off himself—until the Tuesday he went up to Harlem to get some product for rush hour.

That day he had set up a buy at 1 p.m. for fifty-thousand-dollars' worth of cocaine. He had the cash in a brown lunch bag on the passenger seat of his BMW. He parked in front of an abandoned warehouse and told me he never worried, never even thought about getting ripped off. He had friends everywhere and never carried a gun. He believed he was graced.

He had no memory of the assault. He was inside the warehouse unconscious for thirty hours when he was awakened by the voices of kids standing near him.

"That man is dead, I tell you. He's a dead man, and we ought to be getting out of here."

"That fool ain't dead. I see his fat white belly movin' up and down. He's fucked up, but he ain't dead."

Steve said his first memory was the cold cement floor he could feel on his right cheek and the smell of his own vomit. As he spit out part of a tooth, he realized he was covered in something sticky and crusty at the same time. He later found out it was his own dried blood. He was naked and stuck to the floor with his own body fluids. When he pushed himself up, or tried to, the kids ran out screaming and yelling that there was a ghost in the building. They drew enough attention that a passing patrol car came to check it out. The BMW, the money, and his clothes were gone. He remembers flashes of the ride in the ambulance to the hospital, then recalls waking up with two FBI agents at his side the next day. As he was well enough to be transported, he was arraigned and looking at a five-year sentence.

He said the ambush and being left for dead were his "bottom," the term addicts use to describe their turning point in an addiction. From the moment he woke up on the floor of the warehouse, he knew he would never do drugs again. When I asked him how he could be so sure, he simply said, "Because it would be suicide."

Therapy had gone well for the first few sessions. We talked about a wide range of topics, but focused on the effect drugs had had on his life. During his band's tours in Europe in the mid-seventies, he had spent time in prisons in Denmark and Paris for drug dealing. He knew friends who had died of overdoses and, of course, there was what happened in Harlem. Even though our sessions started in the summer, Steve, like most recovering junkies, always wore long sleeves. It wasn't until nearly two months of therapy that I saw the leaf underneath his long-sleeved shirt.

"I see you've got a marijuana plant growing under that fine shirt of yours," I said.

He rolled up his cuff to show me.

"A stupid idea for a tattoo," he said.

"Let me guess, you used to shoot into the purple stems to keep track marks hidden," I said.

"You are either one hell of a guesser," he said, "or I ain't the first junkie to grace this office."

"I've seen it before," I said.

"Was the person alive or dead?"

"Good question," I said avoiding the answer. "What is it like to carry that reminder of your addiction with you?"

"I really don't think about—"

Suddenly the room was filled with a piercing, screaming noise and a red pulsing light. His ankle bracelet had gone off and his right foot was flashing and wailing.

"Holy shit!" he cried. "What the fuck is that?"

"Jesus, that's your ankle bracelet. I've never heard one go off. You really know how to attract attention to yourself," I joked.

"Holy fuck! You've got to let me use the phone!" he screamed.

I handed Steve the phone, and he dialed a number he had in his wallet. He immediately rattled off his name and a series of numbers for identification. He handed me the phone and said they wanted to talk to me.

"Are you Dr. Tomasulo?" asked the voice at the other end of the line.

"Yes," I screamed over the alarm.

"What's your middle name?" he asked.

"Joseph," I said.

"What kind of car do you drive?" asked the voice.

"Toyota," I bellowed.

"What's your secretary's name?" he asked.

"You've got to be kidding me."

"I assure you this is no joke, Doctor."

"Dolores."

"Why did the session go over the time limit?" he queried.

"I didn't realize it had," I said.

"Please wait."

The alarm continued. Dolores knocked on the door, and Steve opened it.

"Nothing to worry about, Dolores," Steve said quickly. "This is my emotional barometer. It goes off whenever I have a feeling or an insight."

Dolores laughed; she liked Steve.

"This must have been a big one," she said.

Then, just as suddenly as it began, it stopped.

"False alarm," Steve said, smiling at Dolores.

The voice came back on the phone.

"Dr. Tomasulo, did it stop?"

"Yes, it did. Why did it go off?" I asked.

"There is a five-minute grace period, but if Steve doesn't show up where he is supposed to be, it goes off," he said.

"That would have been good for me to know," I argued.

"It's in your contract," he said as he hung up.

"That's my whole fucking life right now," said Steve. "They monitor everything I do. Literally, if they don't like the color of my piss I'm in trouble. I really fucked up," he said.

"Listen," I said, "until the air-raid siren on your toe went off, it was a pretty good session."

"Other than that, Mrs. Lincoln, how was the play?" he quipped.

Steve finished the drug-rehab program in record time (of course). He had become well liked by staff and residents alike. He was the model of recovery. He got a job as a salesman in a local electronics chain store and within six months had become their top salesman. He continued in therapy, and his employer's insurance covered 80 percent of it. He wasn't making a thousand dollars a minute, but he was clean and sober and, two years from the day he was attacked, he got engaged to Jennifer.

"We've been living together for three months," he told me. "She completes me. It's perfect. She's ten years in the program and has her recovery together. She digs the Buddha, too. Very cool. Not many chicks get what the Hungry Ghost is all about."

"The Hungry Ghost?"

"The Chinese have this thing about feeding the Hungry Ghost. It's almost dead, has a tiny mouth and a huge distended belly, and can only eat a grain of rice at a time because its throat is so swollen. It never heals, so it can't enjoy the food at the banquet of life."

"I never heard of that before."

"It's about craving. That's what addiction is. Addicts have an insatiable hunger that we are always trying to feed. The Chinese even have a festival for it."

"A festival?"

"Yeah, it's like our Halloween. Everybody goes out for one day and literally leaves food for the Hungry Ghost. They believe if you feed the Hungry Ghost in the right way it won't come in and fuck up your life."

"Did Confucius say that?"

"I think he'd weigh in on the side of starving the motherfucker to death so he stays good and buried."

Steve continued to do well and was offered a job with a competitor. The money was better and the commute from his apartment shorter. The benefits were good, and the only difference was he was now in an

HMO. His psychotherapy would have to come from someone in their system: our sessions would have to end.

We planned a time for termination. It had been nearly two years, and Steve had done all the right things. He was changed, and he had his life back.

"The HMO allows for six sessions a year," said Steve. "That's one session every other month. Let's see. I was in a residential program going to four groups a day and seeing you twice a week in the beginning, then once a week for about two years. I think one forty-five-minute session every other month ought to do me. Maybe I should tell them I only need seasonal therapy? One session a season, that'll do it. Don't get too fluffed up here, but we did some good work together."

"And you will continue to do good work," I offered. "Besides, we can work out a reduced fee or something so you can continue—see me on the even months and the other guy on the odd months." I was attempting to use humor, but I wanted to find a way to offer Steve continued support.

"I'm not allowed to go outside their system—they said that if you do go to someone not on their providers list they won't insure you at all— some legal bullshit—they won't be responsible. So they control my life in a *whole new* more menacing way than the Feds did. If I were to see you for therapy, I'd lose insurance for me and Jen. So I guess I got to cowboy-up, eh?"

I didn't see Steve for about a year, but other patients who knew him well gave me updates on his life. He dropped by the office once to introduce me to Jennifer. She was five months pregnant and expecting twins. They couldn't have looked happier. Steve joked right away about twins. "Anything worth doing," he said, "is worth overdoing." He seemed happy and content. He had never followed up with the other therapist.

⌒

Jennifer found Steve dead on their couch with the needle still in his arm. She had been waiting for him at the hospital with their newborn twins. He didn't answer the phone, and he was one, then two hours late. Jennifer knew there was something terribly wrong. She arranged to leave the twins at the hospital and took a cab to their apartment.

When she opened the door Steve was in his usual position lying on the couch. One leg was stretched out, and his other foot was on the floor. His right arm was extended on to the coffee table with the needle still in it. His eyes, she said, were frozen open. He looked terrified.

The day of the funeral I stood at his coffin and saw the edge of his tattoo peek out from under his shirt. *I'm back in graduate school; I'm singing the New Zealand national anthem; I'm four years old screaming out of control, going down a hill in a red wagon.*

At the grave site Jennifer presses the button on the boom box. The music of Blind Faith begins, and the words from "Had to Cry Today" drift off as each of us finds our way back to our cars, and our lives.

Always Get a Receipt

Blue smoke streamed up from my father's unfiltered Camel. He was in a strange mood. It was below freezing in the driveway and even colder inside the 1956 Pontiac. Another February in New Jersey, and our car wouldn't start. Sitting next to him, I watched as our breath made vapor trails fogging the windshield. It was the eve of his thirty-fifth birthday, and he was taking me for a mystery ride. The *girls*, Mom and Donna, my year-old baby sister, were staying home. For a ten-year-old boy in 1961, it didn't get any better than this. If the car would only start . . .

Anticipation steamed up the windows as fast as the battery drained. The blue smoke settled near the ceiling and formed a separate layer above our breath. The miracle of ignition and a thunderous roar from the Pontiac took us by surprise. My father's smile pierced through the vapor and dreamy swirl of blue as he made repeated jabs at the accelerator. It didn't matter where we were going; the evening was already a success.

Although it was only a short ride, we were on unfamiliar roads. The huge car warmed up, and my father referred to handwritten directions at each stoplight. I asked no questions, he offered no clues. His smile was the only hint that something good was to follow. It was only 6:30 in the evening and there was plenty of time . . . for what?

A turn, then another, and another. Slowing down he peered past me, squinting through the passenger's window to verify the house number.

"This is it," he said.

Turning into the gravel driveway, he put the car in neutral, then pushed the emergency break down with his left foot.

"I'm going to let it run," he said. This was something he had never done before. Maybe he was worried it wouldn't start again; maybe he wanted to keep it warm; maybe he was picking up another person and it wouldn't take that long. Maybe, maybe, maybe. He reached into his right-front pocket and pulled out a fistful of bills: twenties, tens, fives, and singles. I had never seen that much money so close.

"Wow!"

"Lots of money, isn't it?"

"What's it for?"

"You'll see."

"How much do you have?"

"Well, let's see. You get a fifty-cents-a-week allowance, right?"

"Right."

"So in a year you get about twenty-five dollars."

"Twenty-six."

"Good! Right! Twenty-six. And you're ten years old now."

"Ten and a half."

"Right, of course. Well, if you saved your allowance every week and never spent any of it, let's see." He glanced up at the ceiling and took a deep draw on his cigarette. "You . . . would . . . be . . . a hundred and ninety-seven, and a half, years old."

"Dad!"

"Maybe a hundred and ninety-six."

"Come on, Dad, how much is there?"

"Two hundred and eleven dollars."

"Wow!"

"*Wow* is right; I don't even make this much in a week! "

"Wow! What's it for?"

He straightened the bills. I noticed he had a lot of singles that he folded and put back in his pocket.

"You'll see."

Although it was dark out, the house didn't appear to be in great shape. Peeling paint, falling shutters, and various car, bike, and engine parts were scattered alongside the walkway to the front door. Three of the four cement steps leading to the stoop were chipped and cracked. The ripped, uneven screen door was not inviting—but somehow my father floated above all this and seemed not to notice. He pulled open the screen door and knocked, ignoring the unlit doorbell in favor of this more direct approach. A gangly, barefoot young man, not much more than a teenager, with no shirt and rumpled khaki pants, opened the door and let us in. My father introduced himself as "the guy who called you on the phone." This was acknowledged and the young man pointed to the living room.

"Come on in," he said. "It's right around the corner."

Inside was worse. Grubby sweatshirts and unimaginably foul odors contaminated the living room. At first glance there was nothing worth seeing. Dimly lit by a lone floor lamp with a filthy shade, the room was a confusion of papers, magazines, filled and half-filled ashtrays, beer bottles, and blankets. The couch had long since been buried under pizza boxes, record albums, and a run-down guitar case with a broken handle. Blank pages of sheet music with scrawled-in notes and words were everywhere. This room was an inspiration. I made a private vow to clean mine when I got home.

The young man moved toward the guitar case and muttered something about having to go into the service, and that as much as he hated to sell it, he needed the money to pay his debts. His dream of becoming a studio musician would have to be put on hold. Sweeping away the bottle caps and pizza boxes, he lifted the case and cleared a space to lay it on the floor. When he opened it all three of us stood silent. I had learned a word in Sunday school that described what the three of us were doing: beholding. We were beholding the charm and splendor of this guitar.

It was a 1945 Single Cutaway Gibson ES235: a single pickup, hollow-body, electric guitar with a customized black-and-white scratchplate and an adjustable bridge. The young man lifted it out of its case with the courtesy and respect usually reserved for a first date.

"See this silver bracket? It attaches to the white guitar peg in the back for your strap, and it's patented by Gibson. No one else has it. That's what I like about this guitar. No one else is going to have one exactly like it. Around the butt of the guitar here," he turned and pointed the side of it at us, "is your standard quarter-inch plug for your amp, and these two little beauties here are your volume and tone." He referenced these by putting his right thumb and index finger on two silver knobs under the scratchplate. "They call it a 'brown-sunburst-blonde,' but I think a better name for the color would be 'chocolate sunset.' The strings are flat wound—Gibson's, of course—and, if I were going to keep it, I'd replace the machines and tuning keys over the next year."

A blanket had disguised the amplifier as a coffee table. He sat down on it, plugged in the guitar, and began to play. There were no two ways about it. He was good. Note for note he played Chuck Berry and Buddy Holly. I wasn't even aware that my whole body was moving and twitching. The guitar, the music, even the smell of the room added to my intoxication. Finally, he stopped, stood up, and carefully handed the Gibson to my father. At that moment I realized my dad was nearly twice this man's age, and I had never seen him play a guitar.

He took a few seconds to retune the flat-wound strings and gave me a wink as if to restore my faith. Without warning he began playing the same songs the kid had played—only *much* better. He played with the kind of trancelike intensity associated with accomplished musicians. The young man had been good; my father was magic.

Now it was the young man who was twitching and bobbing with the music. He was shaking his head and joined my father in a few duets on his own air guitar. I had been transported to a new kind of feeling and excitement by the exhilaration of it all, and I liked it. When my father finished, the young man shook his right thumb in the air and repeated another word I learned in Sunday school: "Righteous! Righteous!" Dad was pleased and thanked him for the apparent compliment. For a moment they discussed the matching inlaid mother-of-pearl dots along the frets and top of the teak neck, then the inevitable from my dad:

"How much are you asking?"

"Two-fifty."

"Two-fifty?" my father said.

The party was over, and my father asked me to go out and wait in the car. I protested. My father insisted, then softened. He turned back to the more important task at hand.

"Two-fifty?" my father repeated. "That's a lot of money for a used guitar with a seriously worn neck."

My father turned the guitar over and revealed a space behind the first four frets where the palm of the left hand rests that was clearly discolored from so much use.

"Also, the bridge is pulling away from the body," he continued. "It's dried and will have to be replaced, and the strings have been tuned too tight. The neck is bowing."

"What do you mean?" asked the kid.

"I mean, look at the action near the top of the neck," said my father, "and look at how high it gets closer to the bridge."

My father held the guitar face up in the palm of his hands, the way you might hold a child on his back in the water when he's learning to float.

We all leaned in to inspect the guitar. My father held it and used his chin and eyes to direct our attention.

"Look at the bridge," he said, staring at the center part of the guitar in front of him. "Do you see how far the strings are from the body of the guitar?"

"Uh-huh," said the kid.

"Now follow the strings down the neck to the keys. See how close they are to the frets?"

"Uh-huh," the kid repeated.

"Look at the difference!" said my father. "I'm going to have to retool this, have the neck repaired, the bridge repaired, and, what was it that you said you were going to do? Oh yeah, I am definitely going to have to replace the machines on the tuning keys. They won't make it until next year."

"What are you offering?" asked the kid.

"Actually," said my father pausing, "I think I'm going to pass. The more I think about it, the more I realize there's too much work that needs to be done. It's a nice guitar, but I'd have to sink too much into it to bring it up to where it needs to be."

"But it sounds great! You heard it. It was perfect!" the kid protested.

"I am sure someone will buy it, you've got time. When are you leaving?"

"Two days."

"Plenty of time," said my father. "You'll sell it, not for two-fifty, but you'll sell it."

My father stuck his right hand out and shook the kid's. The kid was as shocked as I was, and I realized my mouth had been open for the last two minutes.

"Good luck to you in the navy. Good luck selling your guitar. You take care," my father said, and spun around. "Come on, Danny. Let's go home."

The kid followed.

"It must be worth something to you. You came all the way out here to play it on the coldest night of the year. It's got to be worth something to you," the kid pleaded.

"Listen," my father began, "don't worry—you'll sell it. It's a great guitar, and I am sure someone will buy it in the two weeks before you go."

"*Days,* two *days,*" corrected the kid

"Right," said my father, "two days. I am sure someone will come along who'll give you a fair price for it."

"What do you think a fair price is?"

"Well, no offense, but from the look of things here," my father surveyed the kid's apartment, "this guitar wasn't handled with kid gloves, and it needs a lot of work to get it back where it belongs."

"So, what's a fair price?" the kid said with his hands on his hips.

"Someone might give you a hundred or a hundred and a quarter,"

"A hundred dollars!"

"Maybe there's a blind guitarist that will give you one-fifty."

"You've got to be kidding me!" said the kid.

"Listen," said my dad, "what I do know is that it is a great guitar, or I should say, *was* a great guitar, but that now it is going to need some work to bring it back up. Anybody buying it would have to put over a hundred, maybe over a hundred and fifty in it to make it right."

"I'll take two hundred for it!" the kid blurted out.

"Like I said," repeated my father, "I'm going to pass on it."

"Two hundred is a great price for this guitar."

"Well, I wish you luck. How long will you be in the navy?"

"Four years."

"That's not so bad. If you don't sell it now, you can just store it someplace and sell it when you get home," offered my father. "Of course, it will probably deteriorate further in four years, but—well—anyway good luck with it."

"One-eighty," said the kid.

"Come on, Danny, let's go." My father moved closer to the door.

"Come on, man! One-eighty is an unbelievable price for this," the kid said excitedly. "This is a *Gibson*, man."

"I know what it is," said my father, "and what it isn't."

"You're killing me here!" said the kid.

My father opened the door, and the cold February night came in and joined the negotiation.

"I hope they station you someplace warm," my father said bleakly.

The kid started rubbing his bare feet against each other to keep the blood flowing.

"Man, one-eighty is a great price for a *great* guitar," he said as he alternated rubbing the top of one foot with the bottom of the other.

My father kept his hand on the door knob, leaving the door wide open.

"I left my car running," my father said, "so we're going to go."

My father put his hand on my shoulder and started to guide me through the door. The kid was rubbing his feet together so fast I wondered if they might light on fire.

"All right, man, you win. One-fi-fifty," he said, starting to chatter. "That's it. Ta-take it or le-leave it, man. It ain't worth it for me to sell if I ca-can't get that."

With the door still wide open, my father began the final phase of the deal.

"For one-fifty you'll need to give me your extra strings, some sheet music for Buddy Holly or Chuck Berry, and any blank sheet music you have lying around."

The kid answered yes to all three requests and loaded the spoils into the guitar case. Writing out a receipt for the kid to sign, my father added his final request.

"Do you have a pitch pipe?" he asked.

"Sure. Sure I do"

"Throw that in, and it's a done deal."

The kid went scrambling around the apartment and handed the pitch pipe to my father. My father handed it to me and counted the money out on the kitchen table.

"One-twenty, one-thirty, one-forty, one-forty-five, one-forty-six, one-forty-seven, one-forty-eight, one-forty-nine, one-fifty."

"Th-thanks," said the kid.

"You're welcome," said my father.

My father carried the guitar to the Pontiac and opened the rear door to the warm haze inside. He laid the neglected case on the rear seat. He was beaming.

"I got it!" he said. "Did you see how I negotiated with that guy! He never knew what hit him. Always get a receipt. That way, in a court of law, he can't say you stole it—even though this was robbery!"

It wasn't just the guitar that was electrified. My father's energy gushed out of him, and in that moment, there were two ten-year-olds in the car.

⌒

Some twenty-five years after that cold February night, the blue smoke my father so often invited into his lungs had finally ransacked his heart. My mother and sister declared I should inherit the Gibson, and for five years I kept it in a closet, only playing it on rare occasions. When Donna married a musician (supporting the theory that daughters marry the unrealized potential of their fathers), they came up from Florida to New Jersey for a visit. Brian had heard about the legacy of the guitar and was eager to see it. The three of us opened it in my living room and, despite the thirty-year time lapse, a second "beholding" occurred. Brian removed the Gibson from the case and marveled at its elegance. He played, and everyone gathered into the room. I hadn't felt anything like that since the first time my father touched it.

Donna and Brian took the Gibson back with them to Florida, and Brian reconditioned it, finally, the way my father claimed it should have been all those years ago. Other than a new case and the occasional new strings, my father played it the way he bought it that night. To do otherwise, he often said, would be to cheapen the deal.

⌒

After my cousin Gary's death I found myself thinking about things differently. I wanted to live my life more fully somehow. Things I had always wanted to do, but didn't, took on a new importance for me. One of those things was learning to ride a motorcycle. When I started my first teaching job, I became friends with a teaching assistant named Mark. He gave me a ride on the back of his bike, and the adrenaline rush from the sheer anxiety lured me into wanting a bike of my own. I went out to buy the biggest, baddest, nastiest bike that three hundred dollars could buy: a Honda 360.

A Honda 360 was never known for its power. In fact, you might think of it as a cross between a motorized wheelchair and a lawn mower. Even so, all of the Hondas listed in the newspaper cost more than I had, so I picked the cheapest one and asked Mark to come with me. He knew a lot about motorcycles, and when we got there he asked me to be quiet and let him do the talking.

We drove out to a small, run-down house a few towns over. The place was junked up with car parts, motorcycle parts, and dilapidated lawn chairs. Mark knocked on the door, and a male voice yelled from inside telling us to "hang on."

The kid who answered the door was in shorts and looked to be about nineteen. He was painfully skinny, with tattoos on his arms, shoulders, and stomach; and he had short, spiked hair.

"We're here about the bike," said Mark.

The kid came out and walked around the side of the house. He pulled the tarp off the Honda, and Mark asked him if we could take it out. The kid started it up, handed us two helmets, and we puttered off down the road, leaving Mark's car and keys as collateral.

After driving for a few minutes Mark stopped the bike and walked around it, poking and squeezing and tugging on the different wires and levers. He didn't say much—just sort of grunted.

"How does it look?" I asked.

"It actually is in pretty decent shape," Mark said, nodding thoughtfully at it. "For a starter bike, you could do a lot worse. The tires are a little worn—but that means he's been using it a lot—and that, typically, is a good thing."

"So, good, what should we offer him?" I wondered out loud.

"It doesn't work like that," said Mark. "Let me do the haggling."

When we got back the kid was throwing rusted pieces of lawn furniture from the front yard to the side yard. We got off the bike, and Mark left it running. He began the negotiation.

"What are you asking for this piece of shit?"

"Four hundred."

"Four hundred dollars?"

"I had some work done on it. It's definitely worth at least three-fifty."

"You're asking three hundred and fifty dollars for this piece of shit?"

"I'll throw in the helmet and the gloves."

"The helmet and gloves are both pieces of shit."

"Listen, I've got to get at least three hundred for it," said the kid.

"The manifold has been drilled out and plugged," said Mark, "so someone was making a lot of noise with this—then plugged the holes up with tailpipe putty. That shit isn't going to last for long, and now we're looking at some serious cash to replace the manifold."

The kid just shrugged his shoulders.

"And the tires are shot, man," Mark continued. "We're going to have to replace the tires, and the cables are stretched out. They are going to have to be replaced, too."

"So, do you want to make an offer?"

"When was the last time you overhauled the carburetor?"

"Shit, man, I don't know. Like a year ago."

"Well, it sounds like it needs it again."

"So, what do you want to offer?" he asked again.

"Actually, I think we'd be buying a headache here, my friend. I think we're going to pass."

"Come on, man, it's a great bike," said the tattooed man, mounting his best defense. "I use it every day. It never breaks down, Maybe it ain't cherry, but it's in pretty good shape."

"It's a piece of shit. I'd have to put a lot of work into it and some serious cash. I think we'll pass on it. Come on, Dan," he said to me, "let's get out of here."

"Hey, man, I need the money," the guy said with an edge in his voice. "I'll take two-seventy-five."

The motorcycle was idling and Mark reached over and revved the engine a few times. He shook his head.

"I should have my head examined, but I'll give you two-fifty for this piece of shit—and the helmets and the gloves."

"Two-fifty is *it*, man. That's rock bottom. Deal?"

"Is the gas tank full?"

"I don't know."

"Fill the gas tank, and we'll take the whole pile of shit off your hands for two-fifty."

The kid dug out a large gas tank from the garage and filled the bike. Mark took a small pad out of his pocket and wrote out a receipt, which he had the kid sign.

Mark drove the bike to my house, and I followed in his car. He pushed the bike to its limit, revving the engine when he could. When we got there Mark told me, not surprisingly, that the negotiating strategy I'd witnessed was his "Piece of Shit" technique; he thought the bike was perfect for me. He started teaching me the basics: how to shift, how to accelerate, and how to give the finger. Yes, giving the finger was an essential skill you had to master to ride a motorcycle. Mark said everybody who cuts you off gets the finger. You have to know how to hold on to the handlebars with one hand, while gesturing with the other. He instructed me to practice this for the road test.

When the day for my road test came, I eagerly went down to the Department of Motor Vehicles. They have a special course laid out for motorcycle tests. The first part is largely flat. It has a few turns and some orange cones the driver has to slalom through around the back and sides of the inspection station. Unlike the auto driver's test, no one dares to ride with you. The inspector watches from a safe distance as you start, stop, get off, park, and navigate the obstacle course. Then the tough part: You do it all again—on a hill. It might not sound very difficult, but more than half of Hells Angels wannabes fail on the hill.

I watched a few hopefuls while I waited for my turn. It was quite a show. Bikes rolled backward, some with and some without their owners; some riders couldn't get back on once they were off; still others got caught underneath; and a few got to the hill only to freak out. The freaked-out people got confused and opened the throttle. More than one bike flew out from under its rider and disappeared over the hill. It was fun to watch until it was your turn. That's when you realized you were the next form of entertainment.

I had practiced doing all the maneuvers on a hill near my house. Not once in the dozens of time I practiced did I ever do it right. Although I never got hurt too badly, I had no confidence I could do it. My big plan was to take the test, fail it, and then take it again in two weeks. I figured this way I would learn the course and be able to pass it on the second try. When I developed my test-taking strategy, I hadn't figured in the amount of amusement I'd be providing for those still in line. As luck would have it, the guy who got behind me was riding a chopped Harley that sounded like a jet aircraft when it idled. He had all the makings of a true biker. His beard was made of Brillo, and what you could see of his face looked like partially cooked oatmeal. Although you wouldn't call him fat (not if you wanted to live), he was. He was a huge man whose belt disappeared under his belly and whose rear end looked like two Volkswagen Bugs trying to pass each other. He was gross, and he knew it. I saw him spit, and whatever it was that came out of his mouth dug a hole in the ground. He was the one who laughed the loudest when anyone screwed up on the hill. Just what I needed, Attila the Hun in my rearview mirror.

I did the first part of the test at a whopping four miles per hour. The routine was for one person to go and the next to start two minutes later. Mr. Congeniality was apparently having a snit fit because of my (lack of) speed and was revving his engine. The motor vehicle examiner asked me if I would let the Brillo man go in front of me. Sure. Who needs to be stalked by two Volkswagens and a plate of oatmeal?

He got the signal from the tester, and the big man roared past me. I turned the throttle of my 360 a few times just to display my annoyance. If he heard it at all he would have thought a mosquito had flown by his helmet. Attila danced through the flatlands in record time. But on the hill something happened. This massive life form suddenly looked like green Jell-O on a stick. He couldn't manage the turns on the bike, and the more he tried to control it the worse it got. To everyone's surprise, particularly his, the mighty man and his machine wobbled, shook, and fell hard to the ground. The thud-crash sound was painful to hear, and apparently even more painful to feel. Attila let out a scream.

Instinct took over when I realized I was the closest person to him. I banged my bike into gear and rode up the hill to where he lay. I hopped off the bike, put down the kickstand, and tried to lift his huge bike off him. Others got there within a few seconds, and he was freed.

The whole incident was over in minutes. I turned, hopped on my bike, and went back to the bottom of the hill to finish the test. The examiner came up to me and smiled. "You passed," he said. "Now go on, get out of here." Without realizing it, by helping Attila I had success-fully conquered the hill.

The truth is, riding a motorcycle wasn't what I thought it would be. The helmet, the gloves, the boots, the jacket—all these things just made me sweat. The cars thought I had a target on my back, and every fly, bee, and lightning bug with a death wish kamikazed into me. At night there is nothing quite like having a lightning bug hit the visor of your helmet at sixty miles an hour. The final straw was when a red cardinal flew into my leg and exploded on impact. I now refer to that as the *shredded-tweet* incident.

Between the pain, the blood, and the flying red feathers I decided, after only six months, to sell the 360.

Two guys came together to look at it. They took it for a ride around the block. When they came back the bargaining began.

"What are you asking for this piece of shit?"

The Marathon Runs

When I was six years old my best friend was named Kevin. He and his family lived in the apartment below ours. Kevin's father, Frank, was a rent-a-cop who worked the night shift in a department store. He was always complaining that I made too much noise and woke him up when he needed to sleep in the mornings. Kevin said his dad had a gun. I didn't believe him. We were both in first grade and went to catechism together. I called Kevin a liar and told him he would burn in hell because he was lying to me about the gun. I remember the exact conversation:

"You're lying!"

"No, I'm not!"

"Yes, you are!"

"No, I'm not!"

"Yes, you are!"

"No, I'm not!"

"Yes, you are! Yes, you are! And you're going to burn in hell for lying."

He swore it was true—that he had seen it—but his father would never let him take it out of the apartment. I told him I would ask his father if I could see it. I knew Kevin's father because he came to my door around six each morning to tell me I'd woken him up. Kevin said his father would get mad if I asked about the gun because Kevin wasn't supposed to know about it. At that point I explained that the matter was out of my hands. If he couldn't prove to me that his father had a gun, it meant he was lying, and he would definitely burn in hell for all eternity. Kevin started to cry. He said he was really telling the truth and that we had to figure out some way to prove it. He didn't want to burn in hell, and particularly not for all eternity. I used the words of Sister Mary Theresa: *If you can't prove you're not lying, then you're lying, and you will burn in hell.* Kevin shuddered. He had to get himself in the clear. He kicked the dirt in frustration and thought hard for a full five minutes. Then, as if met with a celestial vision, he looked up beaming and announced his plan for redemption (later to be known as Plan A): he would steal one of his father's bullets and bring it to me.

Kevin actually had an idea about where his father kept the bullets. The plan was for him to find them, take one, show me, then put it back. The logic was simple, and Plan A was simple. If Frank had bullets, he had to have a gun. No sense having bullets if you can't shoot them. If Kevin could get his hands on a bullet and show me, he'd be off the hook. He'd escape going to hell and clear his good name. (There was the matter of his stealing a candy bar from the corner store over the summer, but he had confessed this to Father Doyle and plea-bargained it down to a venial sin, a religious misdemeanor.)

To "borrow" a bullet (we were careful not to call it stealing since he had a mark on him from the candy episode) was an elegant, yet simple plan. What we hadn't counted on were the complications.

Kevin was pretty certain the bullets were hidden in a shoe box on the floor of his father's closet. Two weeks earlier he had peeked through the slightly open bedroom door when his father thought he was asleep. That was the first time he had seen them.

He went into his parents' bedroom to look around when he was sure his mother was going to be out of the apartment for at least twenty minutes. She said she was going to borrow a cup of sugar from Angie across the hall. This typically guaranteed that she would talk for *at least* twenty minutes. The sugar request was just an excuse to "yap"—to use Kevin's father's word. As soon as she left he began his search.

Kevin went directly to the closet and started rummaging. There were several shoe boxes, and he started flipping the covers off each. On the fourth try he hit the jackpot. A half-dozen small boxes of bullets and a few loose ones. He was thrilled. He took one of the loose ones, stuck it in his left pocket, and then put the lids back on. Plan A was on the way to success.

But just as he was easing up off the floor and out of the closet he heard his mother talking.

"This will be so much better than standing in that drafty hallway. Come on in, Angie, and I'll put a pot of coffee on," she said.

Kevin realized that they could talk for hours. The kitchen was right across from the bedroom. There was no way he could get out without being seen. That's when Kevin crafted Plan B. He would go out onto the fire escape, climb up to the fire escape outside my parents' bedroom, and jump over to the fire escape outside my bedroom—*five* stories above the alley. Then he would come into my room and show me the bullet, and we could play for the rest of the afternoon. He imagined we could just run back and forth between the two apartments as we usually did on Saturdays, and that neither his mom nor mine would be the wiser. He would worry about getting the bullet back in the box later.

Kevin opened his parents' bedroom window and crept out onto the fire escape. He tried to close the window behind him (to guard against the appearance of foul play), but it refused to go all the way down. It got stuck about an inch from the sill. Try as he might, he couldn't get it to close and finally left it. He climbed up the ladder to the fire escape outside my parents' bedroom. He had the bullet in his pocket, and all he would have to do was jump from the fire escape outside my parents' window, to the fire escape outside of mine: a distance of not more than eight feet. It certainly seemed to Kevin that he could make a jump like that.

The first thing he did was climb onto the railing of the fire escape outside of his parents' bedroom. Then he climbed up to the fire escape outside my parents' room—so far, so good. Finally he was ready to climb up on the railing of my parents' fire escape and jump the eight feet over to mine. What he didn't count on was sneezing.

As he stood on top of the railing, he swung his arms out and back to give him a boost for the jump. On the last reach back of the third swing, he suddenly had the urge to sneeze. This interrupted his swing, and he instinctively threw his arms up to cover his mouth. The momentum pulled him off the railing, and the sneeze forced his eyes closed. He fell toward the outside railing of my fire escape and ended up with his arm pinned between two pieces of wrought iron on the outside edge. Kevin dangled by his arm five stories above Union City.

I waited in my room for twenty minutes, then thirty, then an hour. I figured Kevin must have been lying about the gun and instead of going down to look for the nonexistent bullet, he had packed his bags and was running away from home. I felt bad for him. In the words of Sister Mary Theresa: *You can never run away from a lie.* Poor Kevin. I hated the thought of him burning in hell for all eternity.

I played for a while in my room until I heard Kevin's mother knock on the door. She wanted to borrow a cup of sugar, meaning, of course, that it was now my mom's turn to "yap" with her.

They sat in the kitchen and talked while my mom made coffee. Kevin's mom apparently didn't realize he was missing because she didn't say anything about him. But she did say something that got me to thinking.

"You want to hear something strange," she said to my mom.

"Sure," my mom said.

"I went into my bedroom to show Angie my new dress from Bamberger's and, do you know what? My bedroom window was open. Only about an inch, but I don't remember Frank opening it. He's a New Yorker; you know how he hates fresh air. But there it was, open about an inch. I guess I'll have to ask him when he gets home from bowling tonight." I didn't listen further because I knew Kevin would have done what I would have done. I looked out my bedroom window. I didn't see anything but the fire escape at first, but then I saw Kevin's arm. I opened the window and crawled out onto the fire escape. Kevin was crying quietly, but in a panic. His arm was swollen and blue. This wasn't good. He told me what had happened to him, and I pulled his other hand over to the fire escape so he could hang on with both hands. As I reached over the railing a powerfully putrid odor jammed my nose. It made my eyes sting. As I helped pull Kevin to the safety of the fire escape landing the smell intensified. His pants were wet, and it was clear what had happened. Kevin had shit himself, and diarrhea was dripping down his scrawny legs to the alley five stories below.

The smell made me gag. It hurt my nose to be near him. He was a mess, and now I had his mess all over me. It was time for Plan C.

Our mothers were in the kitchen talking, so we decided that I should go to the bathroom and steal—I mean borrow—some wet towels to clean Kevin off. First, I took my clothes off and changed into my Hopalong Cassidy shirt with another pair of pants. Then I went to the bathroom and snuck two wet towels back to Kevin and gave him a pair of pants and a shirt to wear. I didn't give him my underwear because it was just too much to think about. We tied all our smelly clothes together with the towels and threw them down the alley. Then we snuck down the hall and went outside, yelling to our mothers that we would be playing down in the park. We disposed of the evidence outside of our building. Then we huddled at the far end of the playground, well behind the bench where all the mothers sat, and pledged a solemn vow to forsake forevermore the evils of sin and criminal wrongdoing. This was one sin we were *definitely* running away from. May Sister Mary Theresa never be the wiser.

～

As soon as my wife told me we were going to be parents, my view of the world changed. I began to worry about things previously unknown to me and started to reevaluate the way I was living. I was no longer going to be simply my wife's mate; I would be someone's father. Anxiety about being financially responsible, more mature, and more mindful consumed me.

I would listen to a news report in the afternoon on how much it would cost to send a child born this year to college and wake up at three in the morning trying to figure where I might get my hands on one hundred and fifty thousand dollars.

The weeks following my wife's news brought other anxieties as well. Will the baby be born all right? Will my wife's hormones change her mood? How do you hold a baby? How do you change a diaper? What do they eat? What if they're twins? If they are twins, where can I get my hands on three hundred thousand dollars?

I decided I would have to channel my anxiety and find a way to burn off the excess energy generated by my concerns. Increasing from my usual 20-miles-a-week running to 30 or so seemed like a good idea, so I set my sight on something to train for, something worthy of all this extra running: the New York City Marathon.

I trained with my friend Bruce for six months. A lot goes into training for a marathon, with the idea, of course, being to build yourself up to running those 26.2 miles. To do this you try to run 35–50 miles a week. Some people run more than that—but that was all Bruce and I could put into it. The goal was simply to finish: burn off some anxiety and finish. But it is of no comfort to recall that in 490 BC, the first runner of a "marathon," Pheidippides, ran 26.2 miles from Marathon to Athens to announce the good news of victory over the Persians. He dropped dead as soon as he got the words out.

When you start adding miles to training runs, things happen to your body. You start noticing aches and pains in places you didn't know you had. Although running is usually considered an excellent way to control body weight, it didn't work that way for me. When I began training I ate everything in sight. I would briefly hesitate when I contemplated what I was about to eat, wondering if it would be good for me. Then I would quickly scarf it down, with the comforting thought that I was training for a marathon. For me, this type of thinking became circular. I was eating so much I *had* to train for a marathon. Once this cycle started, there didn't seem any way of getting out of it.

The basic wisdom goes something like this: train, add mileage, train some more, add mileage, add mileage, add mileage; then, about two weeks before the marathon, do your longest run, something around twenty miles. The most adamant rule I heard was never to do more than a twenty-mile run in training. Bring yourself to "The Wall," but never past it. Save that torture for the day of the race. Don't deplete yourself until you have to. I had heard about "The Wall"—the twenty-mile mark—but didn't know much about it. "Don't run more than twenty miles" just seemed like excellent advice, and I observed it closely. About two weeks before the big race, Bruce and I laid out exactly twenty miles in a course that zigzagged across my town. The day of the run we planted water bottles and special carbohydrate drinks in selected hiding places on the course, then ran it. I felt drained and worn—but still kicking. In my mind, I was ready. The days leading up to the race were filled with light jogging and the ever popular carbo-loading. I had a simple rule for carbo-loading: eat everything white, brown, or yellow. You are supposed to carbo-load the night before the race. I didn't want to wait until the last minute for this sort of thing, so I began carbo-loading two Sundays before the marathon.

On the day of the race everybody was talking about "The Wall." Experienced runners spoke of it with mystical reverence. Us newcomers would ask questions: What happens when you hit "The Wall"? Can you avoid it? Are you permanently injured by "The Wall"? When does it happen? Do women hit "The Wall" the same way men do? Where do you feel it the most? What really happens?

The experienced would say there is nothing like it. Some spoke of the runner's high that preceded it. Some told stories of becoming delusional and dropping out of the race. Some runners told warlike stories of survival and heroism. The runners that intrigued me the most were the ones who said they preferred not to talk about it at all. You knew they had some awful knowledge they were trying to spare you. It was a charged topic, and I was both frightened and fascinated. I put it on the same plane as an alien abduction. Despite a perverse, yet scientific interest, it was probably best not to know.

My daughter was born two weeks before the marathon. Many of my friends are psychologists, and none were shy on theories about why I was running. The most positive spin was that I wanted to experience sympathy pains to match my wife's pain of childbirth. Other theories were less gracious, like the one that said I needed attention for something happening to my body, while my wife was having something happening to hers. The week of the marathon, Bruce's wife gave me a shirt saying "Devon's Daddy" on the front, and "Ask Me about My Daughter Devon Born October 11th, 1985," on the back.

Bruce and I got up about 4:30 the day of the marathon and took a bus with 20,000 runners from midtown Manhattan to the assembly point at Fort Hancock. The race doesn't start until 10:30, but they want you there early to "hydrate" you. You drink coffee, water, and sports drinks for hours to make sure your cells are well lubricated. This, of course, gives way to what is billed as the world's largest urinal: a quarter-mile V-shaped plastic trough that is slightly pitched to move the urine along. For five hours it has a steady stream running in it. Men simply had to walk up to this trough and do their business. There was no mention of where it went. The speculation was that it ran into a pipe that emptied in New Jersey. No one questioned this.

You drink, piss, and stretch until you are exhausted. Finally we were herded onto the Verrazano-Narrows Bridge, where the race starts. Below were New York City fireboats spraying water to keep small craft away from the area. Why would they do this? I wondered. When the cannon went off to start the race it became clear. About 500 fully hydrated men immediately went to take a leak off the side of the bridge. The buildup of fluids and the anxiety of the race were too much for us. If boats had been under there, they would have been treated to a rain cloud of pee. You don't see this on television.

The run was spectacular. Running through the five boroughs of Manhattan without an armed escort, feeling as if you own the city, is incredible. People throw food, candy, water, and paper towels. Others give you Vaseline for your nipples, which often bleed from prolonged friction, and for the inner part of your thighs, which can resemble uncooked hamburger. But despite all this, it is a fantastic event. You talk with other runners, meet people along the way, and wave to the crowd.

It all seems like so much fun and so healthy, until you remember "The Wall." The theory goes that at the twenty-mile mark, the glycogens in your body break down, and your blood chemistry crashes. They say your body is revolting against this insane physical assault, and it falls apart. Somehow I figured it wouldn't happen to me because of beginner's luck. I figured wrong.

As I crossed the twenty-mile mark, they were playing Pink Floyd's album *The Wall*. Nice touch, I thought. I switched into a hyperalert state: *How's my head, how's my heart, how's my sweat, how's my feet, how's my calves, how's my toes?* Bruce had some problems with cramping. We stopped to have a med-unit nurse rub the cramps with a sports gel. In mere seconds we were back on the street. Amazingly, there was nothing happening to my body. I didn't hit no stinking wall, thank you very much, and thought I was free. No difference between the 20th and the 21st mile. I had gotten past "The Wall!" Mile 22, 23, 24, nothing! I had made it. What a great story to tell: my first marathon and no Wall. Now, mind you, I wasn't doing this for speed. They would probably need a calendar rather than a stopwatch to measure our speed, but by the 25th mile we were on autopilot: cruising out of Harlem on our way to Central Park. At this point the crowds started to thicken up and, for me, it was one of the greatest feelings I've ever experienced. A runner's high to beat all runner's highs. You don't feel pain, time slows down, and the rush of elation fills and transports you. I read somewhere the chemicals the body produces during a runner's high are thirty times more powerful than any known opiate. I don't know if that's true, but it sure felt that way. I was elated and floated toward the last mile. Bruce and I were two happy campers.

I had just crossed Mile 26 and had only a couple hundred yards to go. The crowd was twenty deep, and cameras were set for the big finish. There were literally thousands of people to cheer us on. The winners had long since showered and eaten, but the crowds stayed strong. We were running just fine, and I was staring at the finish line, ready to give Fred Lebow, the original organizer of the New York Marathon, the "high five." It was his custom to stand in the middle of the lane as you came up to the finish line with his arms outstretched to slap you five if you wanted. They tell you to look up at the finish line so the cameras will get a good shot of you and your number. Everyone wants one of these photos to remember the race of their lives. Bruce and I were getting ready to give our best smile; I never had the slightest warning.

The best way to describe the sensaton was that it felt like a grenade had gone off in my pants. My stomach literally exploded and created the worst case of diarrhea I've ever had. I tried to cross my legs; I could see the finish line in front of me. *Tiny steps,* I thought. *I only have to hold on for a few seconds.* I was walking like some psychotic ballerina. No good. It was a complete blowout. The stuff just shot down my legs under my shorts and into my socks. In fifteen seconds I had gone from the greatest feeling ever—to this. The guy behind me was only two feet away when I let go. He let out a big "whoa" and changed course. The tiny step thing didn't work, and there wasn't much room to go anywhere else. I dragged myself across the finish line, tried to smile. My white socks were a putrid brown; my lone inglorious goal was to lose myself in the crowd. The second I crossed, some huge guy bellowed out, "We got a shitter!" He immediately wrapped me in a Mylar blanket and steered me off to a tent by the side of the finish line. Bruce didn't know what had happened and was as confused as me when they pulled me out of line. They moved him down the chute for finishing runners and whisked me away to a special unit for medical emergencies. The man leading me to this MASH-style tent had his arm around me as he introduced me to my fellow sufferers.

"Devon's dad's a shitter," he said.

And just to make sure they knew with whom they were dealing, he added:

"Looks like the nuclear type."

A nurse offered me a seat.

"No! No, thank you," I said.

She smiled, then laughed.

"When you get tired enough, honey, you will; they all do."

She gestured toward about thirty people seated around the tent. This was indeed not a regular MASH unit. It was the shitters' tent. I had joined an exclusive club with the highest fee imaginable—total humiliation.

Beyond the mess, the staff were concerned with dehydration and electrolyte imbalance. They made sure I was fully hydrated with a variety of potions and asked my friends, who had been waiting at the finish line, to get me my change of clothes. There wasn't much to talk about with my fellow shitters while we passed the time. What do you say to someone who is sitting in his own diarrhea and knows you're sitting in yours? Then, of course, there was the bouquet, the aroma swirling around the tent. One whiff of this and the term *runner's high* was completely redefined.

The smell became overwhelming, almost gagging me. I am pulling Kevin onto the fire escape, and we wrap our clothes in towels stolen from the bathroom. Tossing them into the alley we find them later on and stuff them down a sewer. The bullet, Kevin said, was in his pants pocket.

And I believe him.

Committed

By the ninth month, Nancy's stomach looked like a mutant water balloon about to burst. She moved slowly and groaned often. At night she walked a well-worn path between the bed and the bathroom. Her normally sweet and warm personality had been devoured by the onset of the third trimester. Now, three weeks before the due date, she was someone very different from the woman I married. I would have been able to handle it better if she was only occasionally tense and irritable, but the truth was she was only occasionally sane. The doctors told us that the hormones would cause mood swings. This was an understatement. Nancy would be okay one minute and then careen off the path of tranquility and scream at me for leaving an empty glass in the sink. The glass left in the sink reflected my lack of understanding for her as a woman, and who the hell was I anyway to be such a sexist idiot? I found the best thing to do in these situations was to apologize and beg for forgiveness. I didn't have the heart to tell her it was her glass.

The mood-quakes, as they came to be known, were unpredictable. In a foolish attempt to do something nice I decided to help out and went shopping for one of our favorite meals at the time: blue-cheeseburgers. The doctors told us to expect that her sensitivity to various smells would change. They didn't tell us how much.

I was home cooking the blue-cheeseburgers when she came in the door. She waddled in like an angry sumo wrestler in heat and started screaming. I didn't hear the first three minutes of her yelling because I was too busy trying to flush the burgers down the toilet. She said the smell was making her sick, and was I crazy for stinking up the whole house with smelly, greasy, cow meat and rotten cheese. Once again, I apologized and begged for forgiveness. I was getting very good at pleading for mercy.

Men have a strange role to play during pregnancy. We are basically useless. The most important thing we had to do for the pregnancy was over in about ten minutes. (Okay, maybe seven minutes—okay, okay, four minutes). Once that part is done we don't have much to contribute. We sympathize, support, and comfort. None of these things really do much to help the situation.

We went to the Lamaze classes and, of course, I was her "coach." I came to find out that the term "coach" is a euphemism for "human sacrifice." During the class I helped her get up and down off the floor. Whatever else I did was terribly unimportant.

At the hospital I asked her to breathe going "he, he, he" when she exhaled, then suggested she concentrate on a single visual point to help calm her mind. When these things failed to help, I asked what else I could do to make her feel better. At this point she asked me to do something to myself that was vulgar, not to mention physically impossible.

I had taught child development at the local college for the past six years. I have a PhD in child development and have worked with hundreds of children. None of these experiences prepared me for the event of childbirth. Nancy, then a master's-level psychologist who has since finished her PhD, had also taught child development at a nearby college. On paper we looked like excellent candidates for bringing a child into the world. Only on paper.

We had our bags packed and rehearsed leaving the house several times in anticipation of the inevitable "water break." If you gather two or more women in any one place for any length of time the stories of childbirth begin to emerge. The horror stories always start with the rupture of the amniotic sac signaling the countdown to birth.

"I remember when my water broke. I was camping in the desert, and there were no hospitals around for hundreds of miles. We hiked back to the main road where we were picked up by a small truck with bad shocks. I gave birth about two hours out of Phoenix on the side of the road in 111-degree heat."

"My water broke in an elevator in Bloomingdale's between the fifth and sixth floor."

"I started having contractions every fifteen seconds apart as soon as my massage started. I had to go to the hospital wrapped in a towel."

"I was in labor for three hundred eighty-seven hours before they sent me home and told me it was a false alarm."

The night of October tenth we went to bed like every other night for the past nine months. At 3 a.m., my loving wife gently nudged me as I lay sleeping in the bed. She whispered three little words in my ear that caused me to respond in a way I never had before.

"My water broke."

I could feel the mattress saturated beneath me and levitated off the bed and into the bathroom. In hindsight I don't remember actually touching the floor. I was magically transported into the shower. I said nothing to Nancy and began scrubbing up under the warm security of the shower nozzle. My psyche was numb, and in what could only be described as an altered state of consciousness, I slowed down. *Way* down. It was as though my entire metabolism had come to a screeching halt. I moved slowly, I thought slowly, I reacted slowly. I remember dropping the bar of soap on the bottom of the tub and watching it as small bubbles cascaded off its beveled edges. I wondered what it would be like to bend down and pick it up. What a curious notion it was to think about having the coordination and the ability to reach down and retrieve a bar of soap. The human body was quite a miracle. I had control over my actions and could either choose to retrieve the soap or let it rest on the bottom of the tub.

While my mind languished in the shower, Nancy banged on the door to say something. It was only dimly piercing, and it did not deter me from shampooing my hair—not once, not twice, but three full times as I read the directions on the back of the packaging. Lather, rinse, repeat. Lather, rinse, repeat. Lather, rinse, repeat. If my wife hadn't banged on the door I might have lathered, rinsed, and repeated myself right into the next day.

In the shower, brushing my teeth became a full-time job. Slow, methodical, and deliberate. Tooth by tooth, twenty strokes each. Rinse, brush, repeat. There was comfort in repetition, comfort in going slowly.

When Nancy had finally had it, she burst into the bathroom to find my hair lathered up (again), my body soaped up with extra coverage on the hairy parts, and my mouth foaming with toothpaste. I was moving at the speed of sludge, a mad dog on quaaludes. If cleanliness is next to godliness, I was on my way to becoming the Pope.

Even the shock of having a nine-and-one-half-month-pregnant woman invade my tranquil shower space was not enough to speed me up. I assured her I was getting out "soon" and eventually shut the water off. Drying myself was an adventure. Every crevice, every hair, and, of course, each space between my toes had to be dry. These things took time. She had already loaded up the Toyota and was waiting for me. When I didn't show, she came back in to the house with one purpose in mind. She would kill me, then drag my body to the hospital. To say she was angry would be misleading. She was the terminator, and I the terminatee. I was in my underwear with my unbuttoned white shirt on, holding two ties in my hand when she exploded into the bedroom.

"What the hell are you doing? You took a half hour to take a shower and twenty minutes to dry yourself. In the last two years you haven't spent that much time cleaning yourself. What the hell is going on?"

I studied Nancy the way I looked at modern art: I knew there was a deep meaning behind it all, but I was just not able to grasp it. Her words were English, I was sure of that, but interpreting them took time. Finally I realized she was asking me a question.

"I'm . . . trying . . to decide . . . which tie goes . . . better with . . . this shirt. What do you think?"

"I think I married an idiot. It's a white shirt. Anything goes with a white shirt! Why are you wearing a tie? Why are you going so slowly? You're—"

A contraction buckled her to her knees, and I was quickly (if not completely) dressed and in the car driving to the hospital.

Riverview Medical Center, in Red Bank, was ten minutes away at a normal speed. We arrived in four minutes. I don't remember the particulars of where or how I parked the car. I just remember getting out once we got near the emergency room. In addition to teaching, I had been working part-time at the hospital in the psychiatric outpatient department doing therapy with young adults who had had brief psychotic episodes. I had been there since the first of the year and had gotten to know most of the staff. The OB/GYN section where we were going was filled with nurses and physicians I knew. They had told me I could come into the delivery room, and if need be, into the operating room if the baby were to be delivered by caesarean. After teaching this stuff for a few years I was excited about the prospect of seeing firsthand what happens when a baby is born.

The staff was great. They knew the drill. Nancy had her overnight bag. I had six rolls of film, two cameras (one for black-and-white photos and one for color), a movie camera, a tape recorder, a jar of NoDoz, and a bag of chocolate-chip cookies. I set up camp down near the end of the bed, and most people would have thought I was planning to pitch a tent any minute. The nurses were amused.

"Going to take a few pictures?" one chided.

"First-Baby Syndrome," said another, eying my paraphernalia.

I helped Nancy with the breathing and held her hand as I counted the time between contractions. I was working hard to have this baby. I thought I would add a little joy to the experience, and so after we had been there about an hour, I suggested it was time for some photos.

"Honey, I am going to take a few pictures of you for our scrapbook, okay?"

"If you pick up a camera, I am going to hit you with it."

"You'll regret it if we don't have pictures of this."

"You'll regret it if we do."

"Honey, I just want to take a few pictures of you so we'll have them."

At this point my sweet wife went, as we say in the profession, "nuts."

"I do not want you to take pictures of me at any time while we are in the hospital. I don't want to do this but, if I have to, I will tell our child that Daddy was murdered the day she was born. Do you understand me?"

I nodded my head and put the camera in the bag. It was 4:30 in the morning; and the nurse on duty said it was going to be awhile longer and that I should get some rest. When I told her I could catch a few winks right down by the end of the bed she made a face that suggested that this wasn't what she had in mind. In fact, she insisted that I leave—for my own good. My wife had drifted back to sleep, and at last I was feeling useful. It seemed that her yelling at me was just what she needed to get some shut-eye. I had finally been of some help.

I wandered through the hospital and eventually found my way to the outpatient unit where I worked. The unit was little more than a few rooms designated for various activities. There was a group room, an administration room, an activities room, a recreation room, and, of course, the rubber room. The rubber room was a four-by-six-foot padded holding cell with a built-in wall-to-wall bench. It was a barren room with a very high ceiling (to keep people from reaching the light fixtures and attempting suicide by electrocution or hanging). It had no internal doorknob or door hinges (people could potentially remove these objects and use them as weapons of destruction or self-mutilation). It had no blankets (hangings); no food (suffocations); no toilet (drownings). It was finished with pads on the walls, floor, and bench to thwart those who might want to knock themselves unconscious.

The rubber room was where we put people who were having violent psychotic episodes. The code for a violent patient was "Dr. Armstrong." If you heard the call for "Dr. Armstrong," you ran to wherever they told

Committed   113

"Dr. Armstrong" to go. I went only once. After I saw a patient cut a fin-ger off a male nurse who was trying to calm him, I decided that I wanted to be one of those psychologists who helped people *after* they had ex-perienced a crisis—not while they were having one. From that day on, whenever I heard them call "Dr. Armstrong," I went into my slow mode. Under stress I go slow. When the going gets tough . . . I . . . go . . . slow.

I was dead tired, and the rubber room was open. I figured I would lie down for a quick nap. I let myself in and fell asleep before my head hit the bench. I don't know how long I was asleep, but when the door slammed shut and locked, it woke me up. A night security guard was on the other side of the door. I eyed him through the small, shatter-proof, two-inch-thick window. It distorted my view, yet I still got a pretty clear impression of my captor. He was big. His uniform was dark blue with black trim, and he wore a hat that was too small for his head. He had enough equipment on him to start or stop a riot, put out a five-alarm fire, or attempt a moonwalk. A two-way radio, a flashlight, Mace, a baton, a sheathed knife, a coiled rope, four pens, a cellular phone, a .38 caliber gun, extra bullets, two bungee cords, two pair of handcuffs, an unmarked black canister, a diver's watch, and a cigar cutter all hung from his belt. The belt mysteriously disappeared under his belly and emerged on the other side of his body. His Motorola two-way radio was clipped on the belt with the microphone Velcroed to his left lapel. I didn't know the man, but I had known others like him. They were all former cops who retired and went into the security business. These were low-pressure jobs that provided a steady income for these highly experi-enced peacekeepers: men with twenty or more years of experience and the battle scars to prove it. These were men with instincts and reflexes that took years to develop, men who still had what it takes. My guy was certainly one of those men. I knew this because he displayed the one characteristic that gives them all away. He had his right hand on his gun and his left hand wrapped around a donut. Not just any donut. A Dunkin' Donuts jelly donut. This was the symbol of a man who had been on the force. His badge was prominently displayed on his chest. It was only partly smeared with strawberry jelly.

Despite his gadgetry, his primary weapon was intimidation. It would have taken him an hour to find and use any of the equipment on his body. Just to see him try and find his can of Mace underneath his belly would have been interesting. But he did have the intimidation thing going. Who would mess with a cross between Grizzly Adams and Buzz Lightyear? The watchman peered through the window and spoke to me through the perforated holes in the ten-inch-thick wall. I had never actually finished dressing when we jumped into the car, so my shirt was unbuttoned, and my pants were on, but not fully zipped because a piece of my shirttail was stuck in the zipper. My hair had dried, but I hadn't gotten a chance to comb it. I looked as if I belonged in a rubber room. The watchman spoke first.

"How long you been in there, son?"

"I'm just lying down. See now. This is really a funny story. I'm not actually in here. NO. No, I'm somebody just like you. Well, of course not exactly like you. Who could be you? You're an individual. Obviously. I see you have a lot of equipment there. I'm a doctor here. I don't believe we've met. I know what you must be thinking. I can't actually read your mind, but I do think that I know what you're thinking. You think I'm crazy. Yes, well, that's a very understandable conclusion. I think if I were in your shoes, or actually, boots, I see, I would think to myself, 'Whew, this guy is a wacko.' But I want you to know that I'm just as insane as you. Sane! Just as *sane* as you. Little Freudian slip there. Freud really knew what he was talking about, huh? Do they make you read much Freud in your field? I guess not. A man like you has experience . . . and a gun. No need for Freud here. Actually, I'm giving birth with my wife. The water broke yesterday, and I took a shower for like ten hours. I know this looks bad, but my wife told me to shut up, and I can't take pictures of her anymore. Can you open the door for me, please?"

A good soldier, my personal security guard never once flinched while I spoke. In fact, he hadn't moved any part of his body except his left arm, with which he ever so slowly brought the donut up to his mouth for a bite. He was dispassionate, aloof, and detached. I had the feeling he hadn't had his coffee yet. Finally, he swallowed his bite of donut and responded.

"I don't know why the door wasn't locked, but I can't open that door, son, until I know what you're doing in there. I'm going to go call someone to make a decision on what to do with you."

"No! Please don't leave me in here. You'll never be back. I have to go to the delivery room. It's my birthday. No, well, actually my child's birthday. Literally birth . . . day. Hey, what time is it? I could have missed the birth. I have a lot of cameras that she won't let me use, but I have some black-and-white film. I thought I would take some artsy photographs and some plain pictures. All the doctors there know me and said I could bring in cameras. It's my birth . . . day, well, you know what I mean. A new baby. Do you have children? Sure, I can see you bouncing them on your belly. Knee! I mean bouncing them on your knee. 'Belly' just popped out. Not that I mean your belly just popped out. Your belly is just fine the way it is. I can tell you're the kind of guy who likes to work out. Or used to work out . . . in the past . . . when you were younger. I'm sure you did some exercise or a sit-up somewhere along the line. Can you open the door?"

"Who the hell are you?" he asked, taking another bite.

"Me? I'm a psychologist. Funny, right? Here I am, locked up in a rubber room with my shirt hanging out and my hair probably a mess and my pants . . . oh my goodness my pants . . . my zipper . . . boy, it's really stuck."

I started to wrestle with the zipper. I lost track of my conversation with the watchman and began an earnest effort at trying to pull the zipper to the top of the clasp. "Come on . . . you little devil, you. Get . . . up . . . here. Come on now. I can't believe this. The one time I need you to shut, you won't shut. I need you to shut . . . up . . . come on now shut . . . up. Up, up, up. Shut . . . up. Shut . . . up. Shut . . . up!"

By now I was lying on the floor, yanking and yelling at my zipper. I was only barely aware of the watchman on the other side of the wall. He was talking on his two-way radio to his dispatcher.

"Hello, Bill. Do you read me? This is Gerry."

"Go ahead, Gerry," said Bill.

"Yeah, we got ourselves a wild one down here, a real nut job. He thinks he's a doctor, and he's bouncing off the walls in the rubber room."

"Sounds like all the other nut jobs down in Psych."

"Yeah, well, this one is hearing voices from his private parts."

"Is that right?"

"This guy is screaming at his dick to shut up."

"He's telling his dick to shut up?"

"You are reading me loud and clear."

"The guy is talking to his dick?"

"You got it."

"What are you going to do."

"I'm gonna hang around for a while and see if any of his other body parts have anything interesting to say."

"Do you know who he is?"

"He said he was a doctor here, a shrink, and something about his wife being pregnant."

"I gotta see this. There's nothin' going on up here. I'm gonna come down and have a look-see for myself. It's not every day you get to see a grown man have a conversation with his Johnson."

"Yeah, well, this guy doesn't look like he's going to be much of a father. The shock of his wife giving birth must have put him over the edge. What should I do with him?"

"I'm coming right down. I got to see this."

I had heard them and was determined to set my zipper straight and look presentable. Within a few minutes both men peered through the tiny window in the door.

"Well, that's enough of that," I said. "I know this really doesn't look good—but I do have to get back upstairs. My wife is having a baby, and I want to be there for her."

Bill recognized me. He had worked the day shift the first month I was at the hospital. He spoke to me through the wall.

"Hey, Dr. Tomasulo. I remember you. You're that psychologist they hired down here awhile back."

"Yes, great, right, of course," I said. "I am so glad you're here. My wife is having a baby and I'm supposed to be her coach. If I don't get back up there—"

Bill started laughing and opened the door. The two of them just shook their heads as I adjusted my pants and ran my fingers through my hair. I thanked them both for not Macing me, and took off for the delivery room.

By the time I got upstairs they were wheeling Nancy into the operating room. The doctor told me they were going to have to deliver the baby by caesarean section. I had taught dozens and dozens of child development classes and had seen scads of movies on caesarean deliveries. But the thought that I was actually going to be in the operating room watching my child being born was very exciting. I knew everything that was going to happen. Watching this was going to be a piece of cake. I wasn't going to be one of those squeamish fathers that freak out during the operation. Not me. I knew what to expect. I was a professional. I could handle it. In my mind I could have assisted in the actual operation. Yes. I could be part of the surgical procedure. *Scalpel, please. Can I have some suction, nurse? Thank you.*

Bill and Gerry should never have let me out.

They gave Nancy an epidural, which prevented her from feeling pain, but kept her awake during the operation. I stood alongside her as they put a screen by her chest to keep her from watching what they were doing. This was a good thing.

I stood next to the screen, and literally was able to see both halves of my wife. To my right I saw my beautiful loving wife with her smiling face happy, ready to finally give birth. To my left, the surgeons worked on her body as if she were a '57 Buick.

The whole procedure took less than a half hour, and at 6:14 p.m. on October 11, 1985, our daughter, Devon Margaret, was born. In less than thirty seconds I had taken two rolls of film. One of the nurses took pity on me when she realized that every shot I took was from exactly the same angle. She finally pried the camera out of my hand and reminded me to begin breathing again. It was my turn to smile for the camera, and I held Devon in my arms while they clamped the umbilical cord, then cut it. For a few minutes the world slowed down, but this time it wasn't because I was stressed. This time, the world slowed down

so I could feel it. There she was—my daughter in my arms. I was en-
tranced by her tiny hands, her tiny face. She was magnificent. Time
stopped, and everything, for a few moments at least, was perfect. The
future flashed in front of me—her first day of school, her first artwork,
her report cards on the refrigerator, a tooth under her pillow, dance les-
sons, the school play, Christmas morning, and sleepovers with her girlfriends on her birthday. I saw her first boyfriend, her driver's license, her
freshman year in college, her wedding, and I saw Nancy and me becoming grandparents. In that moment the whole history and potential of the
universe was in my arms: the invisible threads to my ancestors, the impact of God's grace on Nancy and me, our meeting and falling in love,
and the undeniable miracle that two wisps of matter had joined to become an individual whose uniqueness was about to unfold.

It was at this very moment I realized I had become a father, that
Nancy and I were now part of a family, and that my keys were locked in
the car outside the emergency room with the motor still running.

Journeyman

The boat moved across the Hudson with a speed I hadn't imagined. I was taking the ferry from New Jersey to Manhattan. I dreaded making this trip. I was going to tell my grandmother that her son, my father, was dead.

I took some satisfaction in the thought that the ferry was where it had all begun. My parents had met on the ferry, on a summer morning in fact, while each of them headed to work in New York. My mother lived in Edgewater, the town where my father's parents had their summer cottage—the same cottage where my cousin Gary and I crashed our wagons as kids.

My dream the night before my father's death had woken me up. In the dream he was walking up a flight of stairs to an attic room that didn't really exist, but one I had visited often in my dreams. He stopped as he got to the top of the stairs. He was perfectly calm and just standing there, waiting. A piece of black crepe paper in the shape of a semicircle lay on the floor in front of him. It wasn't often I dreamt of my father, and the dream had unnerved me.

The ferry raced toward Manhattan as I prepared my words.

Grandma, I have something terrible to tell you: Dad passed away last night from a heart attack.

Hi, Grandma, sit down, I have some bad news for you. Dad died last night.

Grandma, you know Dad's been sick . . .

Nothing sounded right; my head was still spinning from the disturbing dream about my father, and from my sister's call. She was crying on the phone. She didn't have to say the words, but she did.

"He's gone." And that was it.

She gave me the details and asked if I would tell Grandma. Over the years my father had come to hate his mother. He had finally recognized all of her manipulations and attacks against my mother. Still, I didn't want to tell my grandmother by phone, and I didn't want to drive. The next train was in two hours, but the ferry was leaving in forty-five minutes. As I headed for the ferry, Nancy was making plans for us to fly to Florida later that evening. It would be Devon's first plane ride. She was nine months old.

⌢

As usual, I am up early and dressed in my Hopalong Cassidy cowboy outfit. I am five years old, and it is Easter Sunday morning, 1956. Fringed black hat, black shirt, silver belt buckle, silver six-shooter (loaded with caps), a belt holding two dozen fake bullets, black boots, and my cowboy vest. I'm in the hallway of our two-bedroom apartment. I have a pillow stuffed on the back of my large, green, toy army truck. With my belly on top of the pillow I fly back and forth across the linoleum floor. Pushing off with my feet from the back side of the front door, I glide down to the end of the hallway, to the wall that separates the living room from my parents' bedroom. As I push off the back of the front door, I roll past my bedroom on the right, the kitchen on the left. I am flying six inches off the floor past Indians and outlaws.

My hands catch me from slamming into my parents' bedroom door with my head. I pull my six-shooter out with my right hand and push off with my left. I fly backward and shoot with my silencer on. (I do this now since my dad and I had a talk about shooting cap guns in the morning.) I fly backward until my feet hit the back of the front door. My pistol gets tucked away, and a few more dead outlaws are notched into my handle.

The flyby shoot-fest is endless. On occasion I am ambushed by a pack of wild bandits and caught off guard. Bullets rip through my arm; I crash and lose an enormous amount of blood. As I lie alone on the prairie, unable to grasp my fallen gun, I realize I am dying. Gasping for my last breath of air, I try to cry out for help but I am too weak, too near death. The light fades, and I draw my last breath; everything is getting black. I am about to die with my boots on, and my eyes are closed in preparation for the last roundup. Then suddenly I hear a faint rattle of the bushes. Could it be? Yes! It's Tonto! The Lone Ranger and I are friends; he must have sensed my danger. Tonto arrives ablaze with pistols and fights off the legion of bad guys. Then, out of bullets, he reaches behind his back and throws a knife into the heart of a charging savage. The savage falls, and I finish him off by choking his neck until my pillow goes limp. Wounded, but valiant, I thank Tonto and get back on my truck.

It is 6:15 a.m.

My parents' bedroom door opens sharply, and I know they are fighting. It is clear from the intensity that the fight has been going on awhile. I have been oblivious to them, lost in my world, killing outlaws and snakes. They are embroiled in an intense, fierce, screaming match, pointing fingers, and shouting. Spit is flying from their mouths as they yell. I'm down the hall by the front door, not yet back on my truck, but they don't see me, they don't notice me. If they do, they don't react to me. I'm scared.

I don't get what it's about. The words are too loud and choppy. Finally they move into the hall. Mom is screaming and pointing into my father's face.

"Why don't you stand up to her for once, for Christ's sake," she says.

"What do you want me to do?" my father says. "She's my *mother*, for crying out loud!"

"For once in your life, act like a husband instead of a mama's boy. Why does everything have to be her way? Why don't you try to please *me* for once?"

"All I do is try to please you," he said. "You're screaming like some old fishwife!"

"So now you think I'm a fishwife? You're lucky your mother let you out of the house long enough to get a wife!" she jeered.

"She's my mother, and she wants us there for one o'clock dinner on Easter Sunday. What is so freaking bad about that?"

"You see, that's just it. You don't get *why* that's so bad. You're so blind, so stupid! Why don't you use your head for something other than a hat rack? You don't know what's wrong with her asking us to be there at one? You *are* a jackass! What time do we usually go to mass? Tell me that, Dumbo," she said.

"Don't you start calling me names!" screamed my father.

"Who called who a fishwife?"

"What's the big deal with one o'clock?" my father asked.

"We go to church at noon, and we don't get out until one o'clock. That's what the matter is," said my mom.

"So we'll go to an early mass!" countered my father.

"Oh, it's that easy, is it? The next earliest mass is at ten-thirty. Do you want to go to ten-thirty mass? Do you know what I've got to do to be ready at ten-thirty, just to please your stupid mother?"

"This is about *you* getting ready?" His eyes narrowed in disgust.

My mother looked like a drop of water on a hot frying pan. She was shaking, dancing, and evaporating from all the heat she was generating. Her screaming escalated, and she began raging.

"You're an idiot, just a stupid idiot!" she yelled.

At this point my father's spirit, and perhaps a bit of his mind, broke. Huge wet tears bounced off his checks and onto the linoleum floor. He started banging on the wall alongside the bathroom, and I could see the tears forming a small shapeless puddle on the floor. I had never seen my father cry before, and it would be decades before I would see him cry again.

∽

My parents, sister, and nephew came to New Jersey on a rare trip from Florida for Father's Day, 1986. We didn't know it then, but it was the last time my family would see him alive. Thirty years had passed since my father's big tears splashed down on the hallway in Union City. Thirty years. My family had moved from that apartment to the house in the suburbs, my sister was born, my father's father died, my mother's parents passed on, my sister and I had both married, divorced, and re-married. I had a two-and-a-half-year-old nephew, and Nancy and I had Devon, who was, at this point, eight months old. This was the first time my family would be seeing her.

The new video camera was bigger and heavier than I thought. I wanted a picture of everyone, so we all moved to the brightest room in the house, the kitchen. Everyone muddled around making fun of my video skills, giving each other bunny ears, and moving their mouths so it looked as if the camera wasn't picking up their voices. They all squeezed into the frame, laughing, smiling, and raising a glass to the camera. Nancy slipped Devon into my father's arm. He had held his grandson, but this was his first granddaughter. She calmed to his soothing voice and returned his gaze. The video captured the tears leaking from behind his eyes, down his face, and disappearing into Devon's soft cotton booties.

∽

My grandmother, at eighty-seven, still lived in the same apartment where my father had grown up, in the West Village. I picked up flowers from a street vendor and knocked on her door. As she opened it, she looked at me, and her face wilted. "Oh my God! It's your father. He's dead, isn't he!"

By the end of the day I was exhausted. The call, the trip to New York, the memories, the plane ride, seeing my father, watching my mother, it was all overwhelming, and the funeral was still in front of us. I fell asleep right away. The dream from the night before picked up again.

My father is walking up the flight of stairs to the attic. This is a special room. In other dreams, at other times, it is where I meet my spirit guide, Peter. In those dreams Peter wears a white robe and a white beard—standard garb for a spirit guide, I suppose. Peter guides me, not so much with words as with gestures and symbols. The room has four sides with four huge windows, one on each side. Each window gives a view of a different season. My father stops as he gets to the top of the stairs. He stands perfectly calm, waiting. The black crepe paper in the shape of a semicircle lies on the floor in front of him. Peter appears in the room on the other side of the black paper. He stretches out his hand to my father. They join hands and smile. With a deliberate step my father crosses over and joins Peter. A warm white light envelops them both.

Raggedy Ann Was an Accident

Sometime after her fourth birthday I took my daughter for a ride in the car. It was typical for Devon to hop in the backseat and for me to put the seat belt around her. Then she'd place Raggedy Ann in the seat next to her, and I'd buckle her in as well. On this particular day it was quite hot, and I took off my jacket and tossed it in the back. After driving for only a few minutes, I heard Devon crying. Soon her whimper turned into a howl. I pulled the car over, certain she had been hurt in some way.

I asked several times for her to tell me what was wrong, but she was crying hard and couldn't seem to get the words out. She pointed to my jacket thrown on top of her doll. "Raggedy Ann can't breathe!" she finally said. I considered my options and thought briefly about explaining that Raggedy Ann wasn't a real person, that she was only a doll, but finally settled on the only acceptable course of action when you've tried to suffocate someone's love. I removed my coat, preformed a short course of mouth-to-mouth, and apologized profusely to Raggedy Ann.

Apologizing to dolls has never been my strong point. As my daughter matured she found it fashionable to take more and more dolls with her on road trips. Although I had no personality conflicts with most of the dolls, there was one I believed had a real attitude problem. He was an arrogant SOB. Previously, I had never considered Barbie's boyfriend, Ken, a rival for my daughter's affections. He was nothing special. His only claim to fame seemed to be the fact that he was Barbie's main squeeze, which allowed him to be part of the entourage on my daughter's travel team.

But to be honest, the darker side of my personality might have contemplated, just for a moment, that he was a threat. A small part of my psyche didn't like the competition from this plastic, phony, delicately built male model. Still, how resentful could I be of a jobless, frozen-faced, superficial, sexless, pathetically short excuse for a man? Him, a threat to me? Never. What could he have that I don't? Sure, he has eternal youth, perfect skin, an anatomically amazing woman to cohabit with, and no weight problem. He *is* famous and does get to hang out in the Malibu beach house (where Barbie has been rumored to be jealous of his walks on the beach with Midge), but I don't believe his fame has affected me. Should it concern me that his first name is internationally recognized, or that he is independently wealthy? Although I am not jealous of him, I do admit that my daughter spends hours with him and only minutes with me—but I am not jealous. He is only a toy. He isn't real. He has no brain. He must be eliminated.

It was a long ride back to New Jersey from our vacation on Cape Cod. I had been driving for 72 million hours. Nancy was resting, and my daughter had commandeered the backseat with her travel team: Raggedy Ann, Barbie and Ken, Samantha from the American Girl doll series, a nameless gray-and-white whale, two small ponies, a blue Nerf doll, and a dingy blue stuffed animal named "Gwabba." Gwabba had lost all facial features and no longer showed signs of any definable form. Gwabba's lack of form was the result of years of Devon's love.

When I started whistling the jingle for Armour hot dogs, I realized I had had enough as the senior officer of the vehicle and decided to change places with Nancy. We pulled over, and as I walked around to the other side of the car, I made a spontaneous decision to get into the backseat with my daughter and her friends. It was a party back there. I am not sure exactly what was going on when I entered this counterculture, but it was a fun place to be. Devon seemed happy to see me and involved me in the play activities right away. For a four-year-old she was already well versed in the art of introduction. Raggedy Ann and Barbie were the matriarchs. The blue Nerf doll was riding the ponies back and forth. Samantha was sleeping with the gray-and-white whale as her stuffed animal, and the great amorphous Gwabba was observing from the rear headrest.

I sat behind the passenger's seat and noticed Ken lying on the floor, uninvolved in the fray of activities. I remember thinking to myself: *Good, she doesn't like him anymore,* and I picked him up so I wouldn't step on him. Apparently Devon had forgotten Ken was in the car and was thrilled to see him. Immediately he was at the center of activity. I was trying to pick up and play with the other dolls when she promptly stopped me.

"Don't, Daddy. Leave them alone."

Her words crushed me. I wasn't allowed to play with the chosen ones. It was that damn Ken; it was all his fault. I decided my best strategy was to make friends with him. Yeah, that was it. I'd make friends with that skinny, never-opens-his-mouth, little punk. I grabbed Ken and began making my best high-pitched Mr. Bill voice.

"Oh. My name's Ken. I like to play when Daddy's around."

The high-pitched voice drew my daughter's attention. She liked the old *Saturday Night Live* Mr. Bill imitation, so I continued in character.

"I like to play back here and learn from Daddy. Daddy is the smart one and I can learn everything from him. Yes, I can. He can do anything. Everything I know I learned from him. He is a great man. I'm just a dumb doll, and I don't know anything. Daddy is a wonderful person. Oh, no, it's too hot in here. It's too hot in the car. I wish Daddy would open up the window to let some air in. Daddy, I need some air, please."

I opened the rear window one inch with the push of a button. I stuck Ken's face near the opening of the window. Devon was laughing at the Mr. Bill imitation and my antics with Ken. She was thrilled with the high-pitched voice, and it seemed I had captured her attention. I had Ken's head right up near the window's opening; then something happened. I went into an altered state of consciousness and opened the window up a little more. In my most frantic Mr. Bill voice, I let Ken do the talking.

"Oh, no. The wind is too much for me, but I like the cool breeze. What should I do? I am going to stick my head out the window. Oh, that's nice. I like that. It is very windy out here; I'm getting scared. I don't like it anymore. I want to come in—"

My daughter let out the loudest scream in recorded history. It was a bellowing, shrieking, panicky scream with no pause or gulps of air. In some rural towns it would have been enough to summon the volunteer fire department. I was so shocked by her reaction to Ken's head sticking out the window that I didn't think to take him back in.

My wife had been driving, but now she was swerving. The car windows had been closed for the air-conditioning, and my opening the window had made a noise and a draft that let her know something was amiss. My wife thought the scream had to do with the window, so she promptly hit the window button on the front console to close it. The smooth ride of the window to the top molding of its frame made a modern-day guillotine for my unfortunate rival. Although his head and body remained attached, they were held together only by force of the window's pressure.

Devon's eyes swelled to the size of grapefruits. She let out a noise that made the first scream sound like a mouse fart. The car shook from her shrieking. At four years old, she had made it to the Richter scale. My response during this split second was nothing short of mindless, and I started to laugh. At the very best this would have been cruelly insensitive. In that moment it had all the makings of lifelong psychological scars for my daughter. After the Raggedy Ann fiasco, I was aware that in my daughter's eyes, it wasn't some molded piece of plastic with cheap coloring stuck between the window and the wind. No, it was a real, albeit small, person. The incongruity of the situation overloaded my already fried brain. I broke into spasms of laughter, laughter that was now about to careen into my child's reality.

Nancy thought this second scream from Devon was due to the fact that some part of her anatomy was caught in the window. It was hard for my wife to make an accurate assessment of the situation using a combination of her rearview and makeup mirrors. So, with the speed of a mother's instinct, she hit the open button for the car's rear window. In that split second, Ken, my nemesis and archrival for my daughter's affections, suffered a permanent loss of one of his favorite appendages. As his head went bouncing down Route 287, I remember wondering if they would charge us with littering, leaving the scene of an accident, or endangering the welfare of a minor.

I was completely out of my mind at this point, my usual sensitivity to my daughter's needs completely absent. She screamed, I laughed. My wife began yelling at me; I laughed some more. My wife began making statements about the kind of parent I was; I gasped for air. She criticized me as a father, as a human being, and as a life-form. They both were either yelling or screaming at me for the better part of the Tappan Zee Bridge. I tried to recover, but holding Ken's rigid, now headless body was both a triumph and a farce for me. I pictured something out of the *Twilight Zone* where you see Ken's head on the side of the road, and as semis go whizzing by it, his mouth moves and says, "I'll get you next time." The next scene is an eighteen-wheeler changing his hat size for good.

By now Devon was sobbing, really crying her heart out. For all practical purposes she had just witnessed one of her beloved creatures beheaded. I made my best effort to turn from being an insensitive nitwit to a simple fool of a father. She sobbed as I promised to get her another head (somehow this wasn't well received), a different doll (an even worse reaction), and then finally a whole new Ken. This was where the negotiations began.

"Devon, I promise you as soon as we get home I will find a toy store that's open and get you another Ken doll. Tonight. I promise I will do it tonight."

Through her sobs and tears in halting, half gasps she answered me.

"That . . . won't . . . work . . . Daddy . . . it just won't work."

"Why not?"

"Barbie and Ken are . . . a . . . team . . . they . . . go . . . together, " she said.

"You want them to go together?" I said not understanding.

"They *do* go together," she said getting angry.

"Yes, you're right, sweetie. They do go together. You are absolutely right. They go together."

"So . . . you . . . can't . . . get a new Ken doll" she said again.

"You don't mean you want me to throw Barbie out the window too?"

I thought she might have been reading Shakespeare or *West Side Story* or something, but this wasn't the case. In seconds the whole situation escalated to its previous pitch. It was my attempt at being funny, but not only was it not funny, my timing couldn't have been worse.

"Devon, I am sorry. I just want to make this right. This is *all* my fault. I made a big mistake, and I want to make it right. What can I do to make it right?"

"Barbie and Ken go together. I need a new Ken doll."

"Honey, of course I'll get you a Ken doll. I said I would get you a Ken doll as soon as I get home. I'll go out and buy you a Ken doll."

"Barbie and Ken are . . . a . . . team . . . they . . . go . . . together."

"Yes, honey, we've established that. Barbie and Ken are a team."

"So . . . you . . . can't . . . get a new Ken doll."

My powers of understanding were not very keen, and I started to offer her things just to bring the situation to a close. By the time I offered to pay for her second year of graduate school, my wife gently informed me what I was doing wrong. She pulled the car over to the side of the road and put it in park. She had been wanting to turn around since the first tollbooth on the Garden State Parkway.

"She wants two new dolls—one Ken, one Barbie. They are a *team*. She wants you to buy her a new team. In her world, the Barbie doll can't be without the Ken doll. If Ken gets whacked by an insane father, she gets two new dolls: a Barbie and a Ken doll." Nancy had the distinct ability to be clear. I finally got the message, saw my daughter's hands holding her own face, and asked her:

"Honey, is that what you want? A new Barbie *and* a new Ken doll? Two new dolls?"

Through her tears she moved her head up and down. She was sad, but she knew what she wanted. She mumbled something through her hands I couldn't hear. I pleaded with her to say it again.

"Devon, please tell me what's the matter. I am very, very sorry."

The mumbles continued. She was sobbing less intensely now, but still muttering, and I couldn't understand a word. I begged her to tell me what she was saying.

" Honey, *please* tell me what you're saying. I know you are upset about what I did with Ken's head. I promise I am going to buy you two new dolls when we get home, one Barbie, one Ken. Absolutely. I promise. *Please* tell me what you are saying."

Through the sobs and tears came a clear unwavering voice.

". . . And new clothes."

"What?" I said, even though I had heard her quite well.

"I need new clothes for Ken and Barbie."

It was my wife's turn to laugh. I agreed to the new clothes along with some ice cream, a pet hamster, a weekly allowance, and a trip to a yet-to-be-named amusement park. The penalty was much higher than I thought. My daughter had studied in her mother's school of family negotiations.

That night I heard her whisper "good night" to each of her little friends. There was a pause after Raggedy Ann, then the sound of determined little footsteps marching toward our bedroom. Standing in the doorway with Raggedy Ann folded inside her arms she bellowed at me.

"I can't find Andy, Daddy. What did you do with him?"

Manhattan Transference

We met every Thursday night in midtown Manhattan at Jackie's apartment. There were eleven of us, ten women and me. All of us therapists, all interested in learning more about group therapy and psychodrama.

Jackie's apartment had a separate room for therapy sessions, but to get to it you walked through the apartment she shared with her husband, Bob. It was spacious, with an elegant yet modern design. The walls were graced with photographs Jackie had taken of exotic fish during a diving expedition and, next to them, ancient African masks she and Bob had purchased while on a safari. This was a professional group for mature therapists looking for certification in group psychotherapy and psychodrama. The leader of our group was one of a handful of extraordinary trainers in the field of psychodrama. Both Jackie and Bob had been trained by Jacob Moreno, a contemporary of Freud's and the founder of psychodrama. It was Moreno who coined the phrase "group therapy." Bob and Jackie carried on Moreno's work following his death. Their reputation for training and supervision was international, and this was my third year in the group. Although I had a PhD and a clinical license by this time, I'd never had any form of personal psychotherapy. Supervision during licensing of my clinical caseload had been extremely helpful, but I wanted to understand the process from both sides.

Over the past three years in this group I had had an opportunity to understand more about how women relate to men and how men were viewed. Because I was the only man in the group, I played the role of every bastard on the face of the planet. I was the alcoholic father, the abusive husband, and the rapist. But these roles were invaluable to my understanding of male-female relationships, not to mention invaluable in understanding the negative aspects of my own psyche.

Being in Manhattan, in Jackie's apartment, gave a warm feel to the training. It made it feel like special knowledge was being passed along in a singularly safe environment. It always felt good to be there.

Then Lulu joined our therapy group. Her hunched shoulders, loose jowls, sunken eyes, and spindly fragile legs gave her the appearance of a mythical sea creature. She sported excessively large hoop earrings, a dozen cheap bracelets on each arm, and a fistful of tawdry rings that drew attention to her bent and wrinkled fingers. The smell of tuna fish and cigarettes ushered her into the room. She careened toward an empty chair while belching greetings with a shrill, alternating, alarmlike pitch. "Hi yuh, Hi yuh, Hi yuh." A one-woman siren had arrived.

It made me anxious to watch her. She seemed to be coming and going, wanting attention yet unconscious of others, interesting yet pathetic. Each article of clothing had been carefully chosen to hide some portion of her thirty (or was it forty?) extra pounds. Her lipstick color suggested a carnival, and oil slicks served as eye shadow. Lips by Crayola, eyes by Exxon. Lulu found a chair and claimed it as her private colony. With great ceremony she took her throne and dispersed belongings to declare her territory. A shopping bag, her purse, a book, and *two* umbrellas. Perhaps she was larger than I'd guessed.

Within two excruciating minutes this woman activated my deepest contempt. How could this happen? How could the leader of the group allow such a woman to join? She should be removed or perhaps shot.

Why would Jackie let such a grotesque little woman into our group? This was a professional group, not an open audition for the circus. Perhaps she was a confederate designed to cause a reaction. Moreno himself had used trained auxiliaries to enhance the therapeutic process. Perhaps this was the case, a sort of psychodramatic version of candid camera. The group began, and Jackie introduced the mystery woman. A dialogue sprang into my head.

Did everybody get to meet Lulu?

Did anyone survive Lulu?

Lulu is a psychiatric nurse.

Lulu is a psychiatric case.

She is going to join the group

She is going to ruin the group.

We learned that Lulu (could she have had *any* other name?) was a psychiatric nurse who had been on staff at all of the major hospitals in Manhattan. She joined the group as a way of expanding her skills so she could open her own practice.

Typically the first two hours of a session were standard psychodramatic therapy followed by an hour of analysis and critique. In this way, each member received a dose of therapy followed by a do-and-don't discussion. That night's session proceeded in the usual way. We took time determining if there was any unfinished business from the week before, then checked in with issues of the day. From this check-in, a protagonist was chosen by the group to work on her issue. (She had fallen out of love with her husband and had started having feelings for a woman. She wanted to tell her husband but was conflicted, confused, and ashamed.) The protagonist identified a specific scene with which to begin and chose members from the group to play various roles. The whole idea of psychodrama is to re-create the feelings of the original experience, then explore them through an enactment. As you might imagine, the experience is very powerful for the protagonist and typically quite potent for the audience as well. Whether you are involved in the drama or not, your attention is usually riveted to the dynamics of the unfolding psychodrama. But this was not the case for the Duchess of

Odd. During the most profound moments of the drama, Lulu managed to jangle her bracelets, drop her book, play with her earrings, or fix her lipstick. Her actions were profoundly distracting, and I secretly hoped the facilitator would stop just long enough to strangle her. This didn't happen. I tolerated this manipulative distraction out of respect for the protagonist, but was determined to make my displeasure known later. I never got the chance.

Lulu spoke up and said she was bored by whole thing. She couldn't relate to it, and it wasn't interesting. She then launched into a detailed description of some affair her friend was having and talked, and talked, and talked, until it was time to go. I was surprised the facilitator had not intervened and was astonished that I had not said a word. The group ended, and Lulu escaped. I felt as if some nasty little kid had just rung my doorbell, left a pile of burning dog shit on the stairs, and run away. I didn't know exactly what was going on, but one thing was certain: there was something oddly familiar about how much I disliked her.

Several sessions followed, and my irritation with Lulu grew. Each week she had new ornaments in her hair and ears, on her fingers, lips, or wrists. A parade of stupid hats with brightly colored gloves, scarves perhaps stolen from unemployed magicians, sleazy necklaces, and on one occasion, shoes that didn't match—not her outfit, but each other. She had an impressive array of mannerisms designed to undermine the protagonist and draw attention to herself. By the end of the month it had gotten so bad I was forced to reflect on my own pathology in this process. I had somehow drifted into an obsession with Lulu's behavior. Not only was I watching, noticing, and loathing her every move, I began to observe one of her behaviors more than the others. I was as worried about doing this as I was unable to control it. I had become the very definition of obsession. I was watching Lulu breathe.

This new level of pathology startled me. I had considered myself a reasonably insightful person, but Lulu was straining my capacity for self-reflection. I measured every breath for its potential to dethrone the protagonist. Lulu was a master. She sighed, coughed, and cleared her throat during peak moments of an enactment. A stifled yawn, an exaggerated exhalation, or a held breath were enough to boil my blood. Finally I couldn't take it anymore, and in the throes of one of her patented sighs, I let her have it. In the middle of someone else's drama I stood up, faced Lulu, and raised my voice. I could feel the blood vessels rise in my neck, and my temples began to throb.

"Lulu, what are you doing?" I heard myself shouting. "Do you realize how distracting it is to watch you? Every time someone is trying to work, you do some crazy little thing to distract us from the person and put the focus on you. Everything is about you and not about anybody else. Do you realize you are doing this?" I said as I stood up and pointed at her and began yelling. "DO YOU REALIZE WHAT YOU ARE DOING?"

"What am I doing?"

"What are you doing? WHAT ARE YOU DOING? You're breathing, Lulu. YOU'RE FUCKING BREATHING," I said, pointing at her and screaming. "The protagonist is pouring out her heart over there and you are over here breathing, in and out, out and in. All different ways, Lulu. You are breathing in such a way that it makes it impossible for the rest of us to concentrate."

Someone pointed out that it was *I* who had actually just disrupted the group, but I didn't know how to respond. I felt that what I was doing was essential to the group's survival, that I was in the midst of rescuing us from the ravages of a marauding psychopath. What I hadn't realized was that I failed to confirm my observations with others in the group prior to using the pronoun "us." The group was looking at me the way I looked at patients in the hospital when they told me they were on a mission from the blue planet. I tried to explain. To my amazement not a single person thought of Lulu as a mythical sea creature or a psychopath. I was alone in my condemnation of her.

I sat down, my thoughts reeling. It was hard to get a grip on what had just happened. How could it be that Lulu went undetected by all these fine people? Couldn't they tell that a witch was among us? Slowly it occurred to me that there might be another explanation for this phenomenon. I thought for a moment and came up with the answer:

everyone else in the group was stupid. Lulu was there to ruin the group, and it was my job to save them. They couldn't see it because she had cast some sort of spell on them. I alone could discern her diabolical ways. I squinted my eyes, directing my vaporizing laser straight at Lulu. Jackie turned toward me.

"Dan, can you say what is bothering you about Lulu?"

Maintaining my squint-laser attack pose, I answered.

"She breathes in a way that disrupts the group."

"So her breathing, which is the function that keeps her alive, takes away from your ability to function."

"Yes, I can function, but not as well as I could if she would stop."

"Breathing?" Jackie queried.

The group began to laugh.

"No, she doesn't have to stop breathing," I said. "I just wish she would do it elsewhere."

I turned to Lulu with a halfhearted plea that she understand this had nothing to do with her, that it had to do only with my perception of things. This was the standard retort in the group when one person had an issue with another. You expressed what was bothering you and couched it in terms that left responsibility for your feelings squarely with you. But even while I was saying this, I didn't believe it. This wasn't about me, this was about *her*. This was about how I would have to inform Lulu of what a miserable human being she was. I would let her down as gently as I could. She would just have to take her self-absorption elsewhere. Why should I pay money to watch her breathe?

Lulu smiled and spoke. "I know this is your problem, and I don't mind helping you with it." Now I was seething. Lulu really didn't get it. I might now have to shift my squint-laser from "stun" to "kill." Jackie stepped in again.

"Dan, can you say how you feel right now about your reaction to Lulu? Can you describe it?"

"I'm disgusted."

"Can you say more?"

"It feels like if I don't stop her, she'll ruin the whole group. I feel torn.

I want to speak up, but I know if I do I'll be punished for it, hurt by it. Somehow, either way, I am going to lose. I just had to say something. It was as if she were ruining everything."

"What will you lose?"

"I know this sounds stupid, but I feel I am going to lose myself."

"So, you are saying that if you speak up, if you say how you are feeling, that you will be lost."

"Yeah. Something like that."

This had become more interesting than I initially thought. How did this happen? Somehow, this wasn't so much about Lulu anymore; this was about me, about my reaction to her. I became intrigued and started to describe my feelings.

"Everything goes dead inside of me, and then I get completely enraged. It feels as if I want to destroy her—but then . . ."

"But then . . . ?"

"But then—I don't understand this—I look like a nut case. She will be there looking all innocent, and I will look like a raving lunatic. She won't understand what I am yelling at, and I'll be the maniac."

"THE maniac?"

The facilitator caught me off guard with her question; I didn't see the relevance, "Er, yeah, I guess, THE maniac."

"So, let me make sure I've got all this. When Lulu breathes it bothers you—"

"It's more than just her breathing," I interrupted, "It's as if she is drawing attention to herself." (Here I turned to Lulu and spoke to her with more sincerity than last time) ". . . and Lulu, I really do get that you are just an activator for me. I'm just trying to figure this out."

"Figure away," said Lulu.

"So, it is more than just her breathing. It's as if she attacks me, robs me of being who I am when she jangles her bracelets and breathes funny. When she draws attention to herself, it's as if I don't exist. Everything is about her, she doesn't really know or care about me or anyone else in the group; it's only about her."

"So, around Lulu . . ." Jackie prompted.

"I feel invisible, yet I am unbelievably angry. It's as if I am split between having to shut down, keep quiet, and get depressed, or get crazy and act out all over the place."

"You feel helpless around her?"

"Yes. That's it: I feel helpless around her."

"And the helplessness makes you feel angry or depressed . . . ?"

"I feel as if I am right out of someone's textbook."

"You said this was familiar."

"I feel trapped. If I don't speak up, I'm nobody. If I get crazy, she'll just say she doesn't know what I'm talking about—then I'll be the maniac."

"THE?"

I was caught off guard again. I decided to find out what was so important about "THE."

"Yeah, that's how it feels; as if I become THE maniac. How come that word is so important?"

"Because it implies there could only be one maniac between you."

"Between Lulu and me?"

"Between you and Lulu now, here in the group—but this is a reaction that you most likely learned elsewhere. Who else in your life seemed to cause this reaction in you?"

I had witnessed this dozens of times before. Somehow the reaction toward someone in the group gets traced back to one's family of origin. It was fascinating when I watched it happening to others. It was torture to feel it happening to me. I seriously couldn't think. It was as if my brain cells had been changed into oatmeal, and my neurotransmitters into molasses. I tried to speak. "Ah . . . er . . . I . . . er—"

The facilitator stepped in. "You said, if you didn't speak up, that you were nobody, and that if you get crazy, she'll just say she doesn't know what you are talking about. Then *you'll* be the maniac."

"Right."

"So if you lose control and yell, you become like her. Instead of her being the maniac, you've become the one out of control."

"Okay, I'm with you so far."

"And when you lose control she says she doesn't know why you are so angry . . ."

A lightbulb went on. I completed the sentence.

". . . and it makes me feel crazy. When my mother yelled at me for things that didn't make sense and I reacted, then *I* seemed like the one who was out of control, or angry, or crazy."

The facilitator nodded. "So you're trapped. You feel powerless if you don't speak up, and yet you'll become like your mother, '*the* maniac,' if you do."

The group had a good sense of what was happening by this point. Heads were nodding as my reaction started to make sense. The insight felt right, but there was still something that just didn't fit.

"I understand what would trap me, that if I didn't speak up it's as if I'd be held hostage, and that if I did, I'd become my mother. It is a lose-lose situation. But there's something else."

"What's that?" asked Jackie.

"I think her actions are calculated and manipulative."

Lulu chimed in. "What do you mean?" she said.

"I mean, I think there is something that is going on with your movements, something directly tied to undermining the attention of the protagonist," I said.

"You think I do things on purpose to bring attention to myself and away from the protagonist?" said Lulu.

"I don't know if you do or you don't—all I can say is that it feels that way to me."

"But you were distracted by my breathing!" said Lulu.

Mercifully, Jackie had a way to facilitate this. "Maybe we have a few things going on," she said. "Let's try to sort through all of this. Dan, what is it about Lulu's breathing that bothers you?"

"It's exaggerated. There is a very slight wheeze, and she seems to take two breaths, then a half breath, as if she is testing out whether or not she can take a full one. Then she takes a full one. She lets the air out the same way. She hesitates to let it all go. It's as if she is afraid. So the first part of the breath comes out as if she is trying to make sure she will have enough, but then she can't hold on to it. It's like the dam bursts, and all the air comes out of her, and she seems surprised. Then she gasps for a breath, and the whole thing starts all over again."

The group was astonished by the detail of my description. Even Lulu seemed impressed. She spoke right away.

"My doctor just told me I have to quit smoking. He thinks I might have the very beginning of emphysema."

I nodded my head. The facilitator looked at me for a long moment with a coy smile, then spoke. "So, Dan, do you know anyone who has a breathing disorder?"

In my mind I see my mother hunched over the phone at her kitchen counter in Florida. She has the oxygen tubes going up her nose. I see the wrinkles distort her face as she desperately draws her next breath. "My mother," I said, "has COPD."

"Chronic obstructive pulmonary disease," said Lulu. "Very similar to emphysema."

"Right," I nodded.

The insight ambushed me. I wasn't ready for it, yet it was perfectly understandable when I said it. I couldn't believe that my unconscious had focused on Lulu's breathing and transferred my feelings of frustration with my mother onto Lulu. I was even more unprepared for what happened next.

Jackie spoke. "So, Lulu's breathing activated your reaction. But what was it that initially bothered you?"

"She seemed to be drawing attention to herself, without regard to anyone else in the group. It was as if we were in orbit around her," I said.

"From what you shared with us in the group, that doesn't sound like your mother. Your mother didn't seem to draw attention to herself. In fact, she seemed to be just the opposite. You said she always stayed in the background. She was critical, but not flamboyant. Did I get that right?"

"Yeah, my mother was self-absorbed, but she didn't like attention. The flamboyant one in my family was—"

I stopped midsentence. *I am at my cousin's wedding. My grandmother*

is dancing a tarantella as the bride and groom watch with the crowd from the
sidelines. In her pocketbook are five pieces of silverware and a coffee cup she has
swiped after napkin-cleaning them in full view of everyone at the table.

I look over at Lulu and continue.

"The flamboyant one was my grandmother. I remember as a child
I could see she had to be the center of attention. She sang the loudest,
danced the longest, and stayed the latest. Everything was about her. It
was as if she manipulated the situation so people would pay attention
to her. Even though she made a fuss over me, I felt invisible around her.
I remember my father telling me the same thing—she made a big deal
over him in public, but it was more for her than for him."

Jackie took a moment to check in with Lulu, to make sure she understood that my reaction was activated by her behavior, but that these re-
actions were based on my perception, which, like everyone else's on the
planet, was distorted by prior relationships.

"That's what a transference is," Jackie said. "We transfer onto others
in the group feelings we've developed in past important relationships."

To Lulu's credit, she acknowledged that she both understood the nature of my reaction and felt I had given her something to think about. I
told her that was the difference between her and my mother and grandmother. Neither of them would have ever allowed themselves to attend
a group and be open to feedback of this sort.

In the psychodrama that followed, Lulu plays my grandmother.
We act out a scene in which my parents and I go to my grandmother's
Greenwich Village apartment for our typical Sunday dinner. Because
I am the only man in this training group, I choose two women to play
my mother and my father. I come running down the hallway ahead of
my parents toward a bowl of fried meatballs waiting for me. I can't eat
them fast enough. They are a special treat made for me by my grandmother, and I can't wait to eat them. Food is love to my grandmother,
and I love her food. As I eat them, my father kisses his mother hello,
and my mother warns me not to eat too many of *those* meatballs. Lulu,
as my grandmother, figures out the role very quickly. She starts argu-
ing with my mother that I don't have to worry about eating too much,

that there is nothing wrong with good food, and insinuates my mother's cooking isn't so great. They start bickering with each other about the food. In no time at all I feel as if I am six years old again. I am trapped and don't know how to speak up. It happens every week, and as much as I look forward to going to Grandma's, I can't stand the tension when we get there. We are barely in the door when the trouble begins again. My grandfather (played by another woman in the group) comes out from a back bedroom to make an appearance. Within five minutes of our arrival, he has his coat on and is taking me out to ride my tricycle. We ride along Sixth Avenue, then take the tricycle down the stairs and on the ferry. After a ride on the Staten Island Ferry, we come back just in time for supper. By then my mother, father, and grandmother all have long faces. At a make-believe kitchen table the group members take their positions as the members of my family. As if Lulu had grown up watching films of our Sunday meals, she starts humming Italian songs and bursting into little dance steps. This is all much to my delight, but my mother is making faces and shaking her head disapprovingly. The woman playing the role of my father has captured the look of his weak smile, and, as if she'd seen him do it a thousand times, starts looking for the *Daily News* to get lost in.

I am speechless in the scene. To be drawn to my grandmother is somehow to betray my mother. But to disapprove of my grandmother, and be like my mother, is painful. The scene ends with us finishing dinner and my grandmother wrapping up food my mother says we have no room for in our refrigerator at home. My grandmother hands me the food to carry, with a special batch of fried meatballs to take home. It is at this point in the scene that Jackie asks me to be the six-year-old—but with my adult voice and understanding—and to speak up to my parents and grandparents.

I begin. "You're all driving me crazy! Why do you have to put me in the middle? I can't figure this out; I'm just a kid. I don't realize that you, Grandma, are just setting me up to antagonize my mother. Dad, why didn't *you* speak up about all of this? This is a miserable spot for a kid to be in. Grandpa, I like getting out with you, but why didn't you say something to Grandma about her antics? I'm sure you saw it. Why else would you have left with me? I don't know how to deal with all of this. That's why I usually don't speak much, and why as I get older, I never like when people do things to attract attention to themselves. It reminds me of Grandma's narcissism, and the trap it put me in."

After this scene, Lulu becomes my mother in the second enactment. I am eight years old playing in the hallway of the apartment while she is ironing in the kitchen. I am making some noises as I play, and my mother tells me not to be so loud. She has a cigarette in an ashtray next to the ironing board, and I notice she is crying, and coughing.

"What's the matter, Mom?" I ask.

"Nothing, just keep playing," says Lulu as my mother.

"Are you all right?" I say, moving toward her.

Lulu coughs elaborately and cries, she knows this role just as well as the other. "Just keep quiet and keep playing. Let me think."

I was trapped again. I couldn't voice my concern and was distanced by my mother. It felt as if she wanted me to notice that everything revolved around her feelings, but when I responded, she couldn't reply with anything other than something dismissive.

The session was followed by analysis and discussion of the process. Although the dramas had been very insightful and fulfilling, I still had a question.

"One thing still puzzles me," I said to Jackie. "I didn't realize you could have two transferences to one person."

"What we did tonight was a generational psychodrama," said Jackie. "Your father picked your mother because he thought she was different. She wasn't extroverted like his mother, but she was just as narcissistic and critical. At some level you knew they were different sides of the same coin. What you saw in Lulu was an amalgam: a fusion of the generational influences on you. Your unconscious saw the details, and tonight you allowed yourself to become aware of it all."

"So, I guess I got my money's worth tonight, eh? A two-for-one special."

Jackie smiled. "Oh, it's a bigger bargain than that," she said. "Wait till you find out that your mother and grandmother live inside you and create the core issues in your own life."

"Are you saying I'm a closet narcissist?"

A few people in the group laughed. Jackie responded.

"Other people are mirrors for us; if we project onto them parts of ourselves we don't want to acknowledge, they reflect them back to us," she said. "The more unaware we are of those dark parts of ourselves, the more glaring the reflection we get back from those mirrors. We see in others what is in ourselves."

"I'm amazed that all this can come from a group," I said, "that we can get some insight into who we are by understanding our reaction to others."

"Whenever you point the finger at someone," said Jackie, "there are three pointing back at you."

My Father's Shadow

In my dream Nancy, Devon, and I are walking, or perhaps floating, into a posh restaurant. The wainscoted walls, etched glass, beveled mirrors, and dark leather seats create a feeling of luxury. We are there for a reception having to do with my memoir. Everyone is nicely dressed, and the atmosphere is cheerful. There are a few people milling around, and I remember feeling happy as we greet them. As we move farther into the dining area there are other people around who are there to celebrate. Everyone seems pleased, particularly me.

But over in the far corner of the dining room is my father, or more accurately a vibrating shadow of my father. He is a dark, clouded mass that pulsates with energy. He is, without a doubt, my father, yet has only a single distinguishing characteristic—he is wearing a 1940s-style fedora. It is as though he were a gangster, very mysterious and a little dangerous. This mass in a gangster's hat is reading my book and looking at the stories, nodding with approval. But his affect, his responsiveness, is reserved. He is happy about the stories, yet there is something he has to say to me.

"You haven't written about my shadow," he says.

The words aren't spoken; they are somehow communicated to me directly from him. His figure has no face, no mouth, no body, but he communicates with unmistakable clarity. The shadow has spoken.

The dream puzzles me. Why is my father lurking, phantom like, in the shadows? He was no hoodlum. Why is he not in human form? But I know all too quickly what it means. As I awake from the dream I am chuckling to myself. My psyche took no chances with this dream; there could be no misinterpreting it. I would have to write about my father's shadow, his dark side. Without it, he is not fully human.

And I am painfully aware that to write about my father's shadow is to write about my own.

⟋

All I wanted was a barbershop.

My carry-on bag was stuffed with two pair of jeans, four T-shirts, a pair of underwear, and a pair of cutoffs. I had forgotten socks, shoes, a toothbrush, and my glasses. I used my glasses only for driving, but never went anywhere, until today, without them. As I drove south along Florida's Route 1 from the Melbourne airport, I squinted into every strip mall along the way. There were lots of barbershops, but none of them open at ten past seven in the morning.

I had tried to sleep on the airplane, but my mother's voice kept tapping me on the shoulder. She had called the night before, and I was on the phone with her a full minute before I knew what was going on. She was crying, and her words were broken. She started a word, and then stopped to take in a breath. When I finally understood, I felt my body start to burn, my throat close, and my face flush with panic. I couldn't believe that at age forty-nine my father had had a massive heart attack. After hanging up I made plans to get on the next flight leaving from Newark, but I hadn't seen my parents in more than a year, and I didn't want my father to see the way I looked. At this point in time I was studying for a master's degree in psychology and working in the field of developmental disabilities. I hadn't decided yet if I would pursue a PhD—or anything else for that matter—so I had let my hair grow down to my shoulders and stopped shaving. I was in my psychology-student-as-hippie phase. I figured a good barber could clean me up in about twenty minutes. I had hoped to find one at the airport, but now I was looking in vain along Route 1.

By eight I had made it to Vero Beach, but still no haircut. I gave up the search and went straight to the hospital and found my father in intensive care. My mother was standing next to his bed holding his right hand. When she looked at me I could see her face was hardened and angry. Her jowls looked as if they were shaped from plastic, with her chin pulled up and in, as if she were ready to scream. When she looked at me I could see her tears with rage behind them. I started to apologize for my appearance, and she cut me off.

"I can't believe he did this to me," she said.

Her words and intensity startled me. She looked at my hair and beard, and then made that face I'd seen so many times, as though she had bitten, once again into a bad piece of fruit.

"You shouldn't let your father see you like that," she said.

"I know Mom, I—" She cut me off again.

"The doctor said it was a miracle he survived," she said. "Just look at him. It looks as if it nearly killed him."

My father's face looked as though cold gray blood must have been circulating through his veins. His head was tilted to the right, and a clear plastic tube for oxygen was fixed to his nose. He had several IVs running into both arms, and his mouth hung open, as if he'd forgotten how to close it. He was breathing very slowly, nearly imperceptibly, and his hair—always wavy, jet black, and perfectly combed—looked like a tangle of old black shoelaces.

I stayed at the foot of the bed and stared at him. The news wasn't good. The myocardial infarction happened when a blood clot hit his heart. If it had gone to his brain, he would have had a stroke. It did a lot of damage, and the doctor told us the survival rate was typically a couple of years, certainly no more than five. Almost as an afterthought the doctor mentioned that my father would never work again, and that, yes, this had to do with his being overweight and smoking.

"You stay here," said my mother. "I'm going to have a cigarette, and they obviously won't let me smoke in here."

"Obviously," I said.

She placed my father's hand on his stomach and turned and pointed her finger in my face.

"You should have gotten it cut," she chided.

"I know, Mom, I—"

She interrupted me again.

"I can't believe he did this to me." She took out her Chesterfields.

"I don't think this was his choice, Mom," I said. "I doubt Dad wanted to have a heart attack."

"I'm not talking about the heart attack," she said.

"What do you mean?"

"I'm talking about what your father did," she said.

"What he did? What did he do?" I asked.

She pointed her finger in my face again. The anger in her eyes became laserlike. It would have been impossible to turn away from her.

"Your father," she began, "your father did something to me that I can't talk about."

At that point my mother turned and made her exit. I had learned over the years not to pursue these riddles. I moved to my father's side and took hold of his left hand. It was as cold and as gray as his face, and it was the first time in my life I could recall actually holding it. The fine black curly hair below his knuckles, and his perfectly manicured fingernails and soft palm surprised me. It didn't seem to be the hand of a journeyman electrician. I thought of all the physical labor he had done in his life; yet for all that, his hand was remarkably smooth and supple. The only place I saw calluses were on his fingertips—from playing his guitar.

"Hi, Dad," I finally said. "It's Danny."

He seemed more dead than alive. I squeezed his hand and repeated myself, raising my voice. Slowly he turned his head toward me and struggled to open his eyes. His breath smelled bad, very unlike him, and his normally clear eyes were dull and filmy Their blue brilliance had faded to look more like worn paint. His eyelids fluttered when he looked at me. He squeezed my hand and tried to smile.

"This sucks," he whispered. His sense of humor was obviously quite alive.

I started to laugh, and I could tell he was looking at my hair.

"Your mother must have given you hell," he tried to say.

I nodded my head and squeezed him back. I hadn't realized until then that I was crying.

"How do you feel?" I finally asked.

"Miserable," he said. "It feels as if an elephant is sitting on my chest."

"Mom's in a bad way," I told him.

He looked at me for a moment as if to decide, then he spoke. "That's because I told her something that maybe I shouldn't have," he said.

He was looking right at me.

"What's that?" I asked.

"I'm not proud of it," he said.

"What?" I said.

"I thought I was going to die, and I thought I owed it to her."

"Uh-huh," I said, still holding his hand.

"You remember those once-a-year-fishing trips I took with my friends?"

"Sure I do. With Frankie, Louie, and Sammy, right?" I said.

"Yeah, well, one time I did a little more than fishing."

"You don't have to tell me this, Dad," I said.

"You should know why your mother is so upset. It was a stupid thing. We stopped in some bar along the Hudson. It was just a stupid guy thing. I don't know what I was thinking. I felt so stupid when it was over. So, that's it. I'm sorry," he said as he closed his eyes.

"How long ago?" I asked.

"When you were a kid; Donna was real little. I don't know, fifteen years ago or so. It was this stupid thing, you know, just trying to be macho. I don't know. I thought I was going to die, so I told her. Maybe I shouldn't have."

"Jeez, Dad, I don't know what to say. Don't worry about that stuff now. Just concentrate on getting better."

"I really thought I was going to die," he said again to justify himself. "It was so stupid, but I just thought she should know. I'm sorry," he said. "That was the only time in twenty-six years."

"I understand, Dad. Don't worry about it now. Just get some rest," I said.

"I don't know what I was thinking," he said as his eyes searched mine.

"Don't worry about it, Dad. I'll come back later when I get cleaned up. Get some rest. Just get some rest now, and we'll talk later."

"I'm sorry you had to come all the way down here for this," he said.

"I needed a haircut anyway," I said as I smiled. "Don't worry about a thing. Just work on getting better. I'm going to go find a barbershop."

I leaned over and kissed my father on the forehead, and we squeezed each other's hand. As I walked outside I saw my mother smoking.

"Did he tell you?" she said as she took a drag on her cigarette.

"Yeah, he did. Hard to believe, huh?" I said without thinking.

"Yeah, well, believe it," she said as she blew out all the smoke.

"That must have been hard for you to hear," I said.

"All these years I trusted him, and this is how he repays me. That's a helluva thing to do to someone who trusts you."

"It was a long time ago," I offered. But as soon as I said it, I wished I hadn't.

"Oh, that's just perfect. Now you're going to defend him," she said crushing the cigarette under her shoe.

"I wasn't trying to defend him. I think what he did was stupid," I said.

"Stupid isn't the word for it. What was he thinking?" she demanded.

"I don't know, Mom, I think he was afraid he was going to die and—"

"And so he could leave feeling guilt-free, while I would have to carry all this crap around!" she said finishing my sentence. "He did this to clear his own conscience."

I hated to admit it, but I agreed with her. This was more about my father's dealing with his own guilt than it was about doing something for my mother. This wasn't about honesty; this was about my father's need to clear his conscience.

"I'm going to get a haircut," I said.

"That would be nice," she quipped.

∿

The barbershop was less than a mile away, but it seemed to take forever to get there. Everything swirled in my mind. It was hard to imagine my father picking up some woman in a bar and screwing her. It didn't fit who I thought he was, and it made me realize how little I really knew him. My image of him was based on fragments of information drawn from bits of contact over the years. My mother's anger, for once, seemed justified. I couldn't make sense of it.

I hadn't seen the inside of a barbershop for a long, long time, and I found one in a strip mall right in town. It was the kind of place where you didn't need an appointment; you just showed up. The barber was sitting in his own chair reading the paper when I walked in. My fantasy was that a barber, seeing a guy like me, with shoulder-length hair and a full beard wanting a haircut, would think he'd won the lottery. I'd bet he had been trying to get his hands on a hippie for years.

"Excuse me," I said as I came in the door. "I'm wondering if you could help me?"

By the time I finished the sentence I was standing next to him. He put down the paper, and I stood there as he mentally shaved my head and beard. To my great surprise he began to shake his head back and forth.

"Ahma no tink so," he said in a heavy Italian accent. "Ahma tinkin you needa fancy shop where dey charge you bigga bucks."

"It's okay with me; I'm sure you can do it," I said. "I need a haircut really bad, and I know you can do it for me."

"How much you wanna cut off?"

"Just give me a regular haircut, and a shave," I said. "That will be good."

"You gonna change who you ah with a haircut?" he said with a smirk.

"My father just had a heart attack, and I think it would be better for him and my mother if I had a haircut," I said.

This changed his attitude toward me, and he immediately got up from the barber's chair.

"In dat case sitta right here," he declared. "Ahma give you back to your mother and father; they gonna get back their son."

He didn't take twenty minutes on me as I had expected. He took his time and asked questions about where I was from, how long my parents had lived in Florida, what kind of work I did, and what my plans for the future were.

"I'm not sure if I want to go on for a PhD; it's a long haul, and there might not be any jobs when I get finished," I said.

"How old ah you now?" he asked.

"Twenty-five," I answered.

"How long this pee-ache-dee take you?" he continued.

"At least three years, maybe four," I said.

"So you maybe twenty-nine when you feenish," he said as he pushed back my head to clip around my left ear.

"I guess that would be right," I said staring at the two of us in the mirror.

"So, den-ah you do it," he said matter-of-factly, "'cause you gonna be twenty-nine someday anyway, and if you don't do it—you gonna say to youself, hey—I could had a pee-ache-dee by now."

We both laughed, and I nodded my head. "That's one way to look at it," I said.

"You mova you head—you gedda pierced ear free wid-da haircut," he said.

"Sorry," I said.

"You married?" he asked.

"Yep."

"You got kids yet?" he continued.

"Nah. Not ready," I said.

"If you wait till you ready," he said, "you neva have kids."

"I'm not even sure who I am; how could I raise a kid?" I said.

"What about you wife?" he asked, "Is she ready?"

"She's nice," I said. "She's a very nice person."

I was married to my first wife at this time. For a budding psychologist, I put a lot of energy into trying not to think about where our relationship was going. Our marriage was at such a low point, in fact, that neither of us had even considered her coming along on this trip. My friendly barber took the cue and dropped the subject.

"What else you like to do with you time?" he said.

"I like to write," I answered.

"What you write?"

"Jokes, funny short stories, things like that," I said.

"So, you got you whole life plan right there," he said. "You gedda you pee-ache-dee, you tell funny stories, an soon assa you ready—you go hava some kids."

"Sounds like a plan," I said.

When he finished I paid him, and tipped him, and thanked him for his kindness and conversation. In turn he promised to pray for my father.

The ride back to the hospital was even longer than the ride out. My discussion with the barber had left me feeling both reflective and puzzled. The great question of my childhood had always been, how did my father put up with my mother? Now the question seemed to reverse itself. My father now brought to the table a history of sexual infidelity and a future that would eke itself out in disability checks. I started to think about the choices I'd made, and about my future. Did I want to stay married? Did I want to go on in school? Did I want to have children? Could I develop my writing? In some important ways my father's life was a model for what I did not want mine to become. He was a bright, creative man who never finished high school and never really pressed forward to develop his intelligence or creativity. I always felt he could have been a professional musician, or even a doctor if he had pushed himself. Forever I had aligned myself with my father and wanted to be like him in so many ways. Now, it was something I feared. To be like him, or not like him: Were these my only choices?

Often, when I struggled with my thoughts, I'd found myself stroking my beard, my right thumb on one side, and index and middle fingers on the other. As I drove back to the hospital my right hand again found its way to my chin, but all I could feel was smoothly shaved skin.

The Smoke Clears

After eight rings she answers. Gasping and wheezing, she whispers the only two words she can manage: "You talk," she says. Eleven hundred miles away in mind and space, my monologue continues as she struggles to find a rhythm for her breath. Two or three minutes have gone by, depending on the distance she has traveled to the phone. I picture her in my mind's eye. She is hunched over the phone on the kitchen counter in an immaculate two-bedroom condo. It is a sterile, serene white. The "snowbirds" have left. Having survived my father, she is alone in Florida by intention and circumstance. Oxygen is secured to her nose by an elastic band around her head. A fifty-foot line tethers her to a tank, the size of a small torpedo, in her bedroom. Her leather face has uniquely unattractive wrinkles from fifty years of smoking. These deep insults streak from her mouth and distort her face. Her lifeless light brown hair is permanently in place. In contrast, her all-knowing, all-seeing glacial blue eyes are on the verge of liquefying. She has no thought other than her next breath; my mother is a bit of human flotsam from the tobacco industry's insidious betrayal of its consumers. She is dying.

Her disease is called chronic obstructive pulmonary disease, or COPD. An emphysema-like lung disorder that has robbed her of all but 10 percent of her lung power. The disease was made possible by three-quarters of a million cigarettes over six decades. She smoked about one cigarette every twenty-four minuets of her waking life. For my mother a cigarette wasn't a luxury or a momentary pleasure; it was a way of life, and, in full circle, had become a way of death.

All the while growing up I never realized her smoking was a problem. My mother's smoking was so obvious it was invisible. Her need to smoke was so woven into her daily routine that it is now hard to recall scenes where cigarettes were not included: dinner, birthdays, dessert, breakfast, Sundays, always. An ashtray in every room, matches on every table. These items are gone now, replaced by beautifully boxed tissues— a battalion of paper gauze to catch bloody phlegm that comes up suddenly, unannounced.

My father had smoked at the same insane pace, and for ten of his sixteen waking hours he did it at work and in the car. So overjoyed at the first family car with a cigarette lighter, he exclaimed, "How much better could life get?" I was nine years old at the time.

Only as an adult with years of therapy experience was I able to see the pure addiction that smoking was for them. My mother smoked to medicate her anger and depression. She used nicotine rather than narcotics and bought it in packs rather than nickel-and-dime bags, but it served the same purpose. She wanted to keep from knowing her rage and her despair, to mask the sense of helplessness inherited from her family. Nicotine became her inoculation to emotional pain, a thin generational prophylactic between her disappointment as a child and her opportunity as an adult. As a parent she could attempt to do for her children what wasn't done for her. It was everything she could do to keep her father's rage and her mother's negligence from infecting her relationship with me and, later, with my sister. Nicotine offered hope through compulsion and survival through numbing. Salvation was never more than twenty-four minutes away.

Hospice gives her two weeks. I call her for ten minutes between her morphine and painkiller doses. She is groggy, but lucid. I tell her I am coming down to see her, and she says okay. Last week she told me not to come; if I came, it would mean she was dying. She says she is tired and wants to rest. I tell her I love her. She says she loves me.

I can hear her on the other end of the phone wheezing, each breath sounding like her last. I am filling the time with chatter. I don't mention anything of importance. For years I've known she can't respond in a way that isn't somehow critical, so rather than frustrate both of us, I keep our conversations light. My mother had survived physical and emotional brutality from her parents during childhood and then dedicated herself to not doing that to her children. But decades of being made to feel wrong took their toll, and she couldn't help but criticize. She had successfully prevented herself from passing on the physical abuse, but the stream of criticism was endless. She hated that part of her personality and would withdraw from others, me included, to keep from being critical. But whatever protects inhibits. In closing herself off from the potential abuses of the world, my mother lost the ability to let love in, or out.

Now I am doing to her what she has done to me. We were both protecting ourselves from being hurt. In the last days of her life my mother is drawing back into herself; and I feel myself doing the same.

In the ten minutes we are on the phone her breathing has improved. I talk continuously, inanely, about everything and nothing. She punctuates my monologue with "oh" or "hmmm," but isn't engaged. I am the background noise to her drama, wallpaper in her theater. Her speech is slurred from the morphine. Finally she has enough strength and speaks.

"Are you happy?" she says.

This takes me by surprise. I am not used to her asking how I feel and don't understand why she is asking this now.

"Well, I'm not happy about how you're feeling. I wish you were doing better," I say. "It must be hard for you."

"No. I mean do you have a happy life?"

She has caught me off guard, but I answer the question.

"Sure, sure. Of course," I say. "Things are fine, everything is going just fine."

"That's good. It's important to me that you are happy."

She begins to cough. I hear the phone drop and the rub of tissues as they came out of the box. I've heard these coughing jags before. This one goes on for several minutes before she is able to come back to the phone.

"I'm sorry you're feeling so bad," I say.

"Me too," she says in a near whisper.

Her breathing was more labored. I tell her I want her to save her energy and not talk, and that I am going to hang up, call her later, and see her on Saturday.

"Okay," she says.

Then I pause, choosing each of my words carefully.

"Mom?"

"What?"

"You know I love you, and I know you love me. You raised two happy kids; you don't do that without doing something right."

"Did I really?"

The coughing jag starts again, and a hospice worker comes on the phone to tell me they have to attend to my mother.

We never speak again.

⟲

I cannot breathe. From a dead sleep I sit up in my bed in a panic, terrorized and speechless. I am shaking, or rather my left shoulder is shaking, humming, twitching with a vibration foreign to me. I can't make myself breathe. My mouth is open, straining to take in air, but nothing. The alarm, the raw panic is beyond me. I have no index for this experience. A vibration is inside my left shoulder: a heart attack? But it doesn't feel like my heart. The vibration is violent. What would a heart attack feel like? Maybe it feels like this. Maybe I am dying. I have to breathe. What is happening? What is this twitch in my shoulder? My father's heart attack happened at forty-nine. I'm forty-nine. I'm scared. *Dear God, help me. Please, let me breathe.*

An electrical cord—black, thick, and long—is being yanked right out of me. It had been firmly attached, plugged into my shoulder since birth. It feels umbilical. A brief flash of my conversation with my mother, only hours before, passes quickly through my mind. The twitching rumble began the moment it was unplugged and stopped my breathing. I am on my own without it. No power, no life, no existence. The humming twitch in my shoulder continues, and I am not breathing. But I was sleeping, wasn't I? Perhaps I am dreaming, wobbling between realities. I don't really have an electrical cord coming out of my left shoulder, do I? But what is twitching? Maybe this quiver has simply woken me up. I have no pain now; maybe this is a dream. But why this dream? This cord gave me life. It was my power source, and it is gone.

All at once the panic cracks. Like balloons suddenly inflated, my lungs fill. Oxygen moves in and out. The flow steadies. I am at peace, calm. As I drift back to sleep, I realize the cord has not been supplying, but rather demanding and depleting energy, for a long time.

～

I got up out of my chair and sat on the end of the couch and became my mother again.

"You're saying I was the worst mother in the world, and I'm not supposed to have a reaction?"

I said these words from her position, literally sitting in a chair I designated as "hers" in my one-person role play. I sat there and struggled to identify exactly what she would be feeling, and the very words she would use. Psychodramatists call this a monodrama, but this was clearly my mama drama.

Even though I was playing the role of my mother, she was doing the same old crap to me. I didn't want to get angry, but I wasn't going to let her get away with it. I got up off the couch and sat back in my padded red chair.

"I am more like you than I care to admit," I offered from my own role.

I then continued going back and forth, playing both roles of the dialogue.

"How are you like me?" she replied.

"I am angry a lot of the time. I feel resentful of others, and I sometimes have a hard time tolerating people," I said.

"That's how you see me?" she said.

When I sat back in my red chair, I tried to imagine what she would look like if she were really sitting across from me on the end of my couch. I'd see her wrinkles, nearly scars, around her mouth with heavy makeup trying to hide the decades of smoking. She'd have on a white blouse—I don't think she owned another color—and a beige skirt with matching shoes and belt and pocketbook. Her posture would be straight, but unnatural, and every hair would be perfectly in place and dyed auburn brown.

"You were always angry at someone or something," I said. "Always! In all the time I was growing up I can only remember a few, very few instances when you were smiling. Every day you were angry. Every time someone got close to you, or started to, you found some reason to get angry with them and distance yourself. Even *I* felt as though I had to protect myself from you," I said.

"But all I did was love you!" she cried, with her palms turned upward.

"But it felt as if you were angry and critical. I felt you only loved me when I did the right thing, and I certainly couldn't do anything that would have embarrassed you. I think you would have disowned me," I said.

I help people perform their psychodramas every day. Every day I ask people to have conversations with those with whom they have unfinished business, but doing it alone, at home in my writing room, was something else.

"How can you say all this? I did everything a mother is supposed to do, and this is how you repay me!"

I could sense all the old feelings come up inside me. She was about to guilt me into dropping the point altogether, and I wanted her to know I wasn't backing down.

"This is why we never talked when you were alive," I pressed on. "Here I am trying to talk to you about how I feel, and all you can do is think of how hurt you are. That was the trap. If I tried to explain what was going on for me, it all of a sudden became all about you, and I was out of the loop. Then it wasn't about how I felt, but about how I was hurting *you* with what I was saying.

"We never got to talk about this stuff," I continued. "If you felt you were going to be hurt, you just got angry and that was the end of it. You got angry, and that was supposed to make me feel so guilty for bringing it up that I didn't bring it up again for a long, long time."

"Danny, what do you want from me?" she asked.

"I don't even know," I said, considering my words, "but I feel as though I'm like you in a lot of ways, and I can't stand it."

"So you want me to help you be less like me?" she said with a sarcastic tone.

"I guess I just want to understand what is going on. On the outside it feels as if I can handle things. I love Nancy and Devon, I have good friends, and I like the kind of work I do. But I feel I am always ready to be angry. I feel resentment when I think I am giving out too much and others aren't giving back enough," I said surprising myself.

"What makes you so angry?" she asked.

"I don't know!" I said as I shrugged my shoulders. "I guess I was hoping you would help me with that!"

"How would I know what is making you angry?" she said, throwing her hands up.

"When I get like this it doesn't feel like me, it doesn't feel as though these feelings belong to me. It feels like your stuff," I said groping my way through these new ideas.

"That's ridiculous! How could my anger and resentment be yours? I don't understand that," she said.

"I don't know. All I know is that I get a feeling inside of me as if I want to protect something. If I can get angry enough, I can protect myself from something."

"Me?" she questioned.

"No. You're dead," I said as soon as I got back in my chair. " I don't feel as though I have to protect myself from you any longer. But maybe I'm afraid I'll become like you if I let those feelings out as you did."

I stayed in my chair trying to absorb the words I'd just said to her. After a moment I went over to sit on the couch and answered as I thought she would.

"So you're not afraid of me; you're afraid you'll become *like* me if you get angry like I did, is that it?" she clarified.

"Yeah, something like that."

"Why would it be so bad to be me?" she asked.

"You didn't even like yourself! You had no friends, and you seemed to have no joy in your life. You treated your own daughter terribly. You made unrealistic demands on Donna all the time. She had her own family, her own business, and you demanded she do things for you that took up an enormous amount of time, and you barely acknowledged what she did for you," I said raising my voice.

"Everybody thought your father was the good guy, and that I was the maniac. Well, let me tell you, your father was no saint," she said, pointing her finger.

I am in Jackie's group, standing, yelling, and pointing my finger at Lulu.

"You see, here we are talking about stuff that you do, or did, and you want to change the subject to shift the blame elsewhere. I wasn't talking about Dad. I was talking about you. I never said he was a saint," I said, challenging her.

"But that's the way it always comes out. He was Mr. Nice Guy, and I was the shrew. It wasn't fair that I had to do all the discipline with you; I had to make you be responsible for yourself. He could just come home from work and be the good guy. It isn't easy competing with a saint."

"My point, Mom, was that you pushed everybody away. Even your best friend, Roxanne. She was the sweetest woman in the world and remained your friend even when you treated her horribly, and I don't think you ever realized how hard she tried to be close to you. Everybody else just let you stew in your own juices."

Mom knew I was right about that, and I sat on the couch as her for a moment before answering.

"What do you want me to do?" she finally said.

"I don't know. I guess it's like what you said before. If I have the same angry, resentful feelings you had, I'll become like you, but if I try not to have them—that just makes me worse."

It was time to sit in my chair for a moment. I was trying to let the words I'd just spoken sink in. It was mind-boggling to realize what I was doing. I was having a full-tilt argument with my dead mother, out loud, and moving around from chair to couch to play both parts. This wouldn't be easy to explain to the neighbors. Eventually I got up and sat on the couch again.

"So, it isn't really me you are afraid of becoming," she said. "You're afraid of having feelings that are like the ones I used to have. You saw what they did to me, and you dedicated yourself to not having them," she clarified.

"Isn't that the same thing?" I asked. "What's the difference if I become like you, or have the same feelings as you?"

There would have been a smugness on her face; I could feel it as I sat on the couch and became her. It was one of those rare times when my mother wasn't just being argumentative; she had something important to say, and she knew she was right about it. Her gel-blue eyes would have become electrified, and she would have burned her point home.

"You're the one who brought up the fact that I'm dead. Everything you are dealing with is inside of you."

I stayed seated on the couch as my mother. That was it! I accused her of blaming others, yet I had been blaming her instead of taking responsibility for myself. I went back to sitting in my red chair to make this clear.

"So, you're saying it's *my* anger, *my* resentment, and *my* lack of tolerance—and that I'm afraid I'll handle them in the same way you did. That's what scares me."

The answer came so fast I barely got up from my chair. "Right," was all she said.

"So, what I have to do is take responsibility for my own negative feelings," I continued. "Acknowledge them, and then realize I have a choice in how I deal with them. I don't have to react to them the same way you did."

"No one ever taught me how to deal with my feelings," she said. "When I got angry at someone I just curled up into a ball."

"A ball with spikes," I added.

"You could put it that way," she smiled.

This was the other side of her. When I made a good point she could sense it and acknowledge it.

"If I let myself really feel all those negative feelings, they would destroy me," I said.

"That's because they did destroy me, but they don't have to do that to you. You are trying to find a way of coping with them. That's something I never did. I always blamed someone or something else for what I was feeling. It was Roxanne's fault, or your father's fault, or Donna's fault, or your fault. I never let myself try to get to the pain underneath the anger. That's why I never dealt with it. It was never mine. It was always someone else's doing. I was being victimized, and I had a right to be angry."

Moving back to my seat, I nodded. "So, I'm afraid I'll do the same thing."

"I think you are doing the same thing right now," she said, "and that's what scares you. You've been trying very hard to point the finger at me, but the better part of you knows that won't work."

"So, if I keep blaming my angry feelings on you," I said, "I don't have to acknowledge that they're *my* negative feelings. I can keep feeling victimized by you and your negativity, instead of realizing I have to deal with these feelings myself."

"Sounds right," she said.

"You know, Mom, I really wish we could have had one of these talks when you were alive."

I sat looking at the empty space near the end of the couch. It was as though I could feel her, sense her hair, her white blouse, and beige shoes. Our relationship felt softer somehow after this talk. I changed seats for the last time and sat on the end of the couch.

"So do I, Danny. So do I."

Reiki

Marilynne stood next to me and pressed her hands together to say a silent prayer. The prayer surprised me, but I said nothing. As I sat in my chair, she cupped her hands as if to warm them over a small flame and let them hover a few inches above my right forearm. While her hands floated, her thumbs were tucked under her palms. She closed her eyes to meditate, and after only a minute or so, she exhaled purposefully and placed both her hands several inches above my head. With one hand in front of my body and the other behind, she gracefully let her arms drift toward the floor. When her hands had gone down past my knees she repeated the gesture, this time moving her arms along the sides of my body.

"Marilynne," I said, "what are you doing?"

"I'm smoothing your aura."

"Is it wrinkled?"

"Just part of the ritual," she said.

I thanked her, but wasn't sure for what. I didn't know I had an aura, much less that it needed smoothing.

Marilynne was "treating" the worst case of poison ivy I'd ever had. It began as a red area along my right arm, then gave way to an oozing, itchy, skin eruption that seemed to percolate. Medicine had not worked, and Marilynne, one of my group-therapy trainees, had studied Reiki and asked if she could treat it. I knew only that Reiki had something to do with energy and something to do with God. *Why not?* I thought.

"Let 'er rip," I told Marilynne.

An hour after the treatment the affected area, so impervious to medicine, had dried out. By the end of the second hour dramatic differences had taken place. The eruptions eased, and the size of the region had shrunk considerably. As the warm August evening passed, my arm continued to heal before my eyes. Skin would dry, then flake off. By the time I woke up the next morning, there was only a faint outline of where the condition had been. Twenty-four hours after the "treatment," the rash from the poison ivy was completely gone. Not improved: gone.

⌒

The weeks following my mother's death in October were emotionally and physically draining. At her funeral it was obvious that she'd had very few friends and, other than family, no one was able to provide a story or an amusing anecdote. The dream from the night before her death reverberated in my mind. I had felt her life force unplug from me in the image of my father's trade; an electrical cord that had been attached to my shoulder was withdrawn in a quick cosmic yank, and some of my guts went along with it.

I hadn't yet been able to reconcile the feelings and the imagery from that night. The weeks passed; my sister and I dealt with the mechanics of selling my mother's condo and sorting through her belongings. Because my sister lived within a mile of our mother's home in Florida, she took on the bulk of these joyless tasks.

By the time the New Year had come, my energy level was low, and I was fighting off the flu. I remembered how impressed I had been with the Reiki treatment months earlier, and wondered if another session might help. Maureen was a professional whom I had known for nearly fifteen years, and although we referred clients to each other, we didn't know one another very well. After Marilynne's treatment, she told me that Maureen not only knew Reiki but also taught it. When I called to set up an appointment, Maureen informed me that the two syllables, "rei," and "ki," refer to "God" and "energy," and that the "ki" part is similar to the Eastern term, "chi," for energy.

I had met Maureen in the past and was impressed with her positive attitude. She seemed to give off some kind of vibration that made me feel happy to be near her. She had a strong, steady, honest smile and buoyant energy. My appointment was scheduled for 8 p.m. at a retreat center several miles from my office. Her modest athletic frame and smooth round face ushered me into a small room on the second floor of the brick building. The central feature of this room was a massage table that filled up nearly half the room's allotted space. A small bed, a four-drawer dresser, and a pedestal sink took up the rest of the room. The dresser's lamp provided the only source of light with no more than a 40- or 50-watt bulb. Maureen explained that I should remove my watch and belt, as they serve as detractors from the energy, and, if I wished, I could remove my shoes.

I sit on the massage table and swivel my legs around to lie down. Maureen tucks a small rounded pillow underneath my knees to help support my back, then Maureen, like Marilynne, begins with a prayer. This was less of a surprise to me given the fact that Maureen was "Sister" Maureen. Professionally I often referred people to her if they needed help with spiritual issues as Maureen conducts something called "spiritual direction": helping people with their relationship with God.

The "treatment" began with Maureen placing her hands on the middle of my stomach, on my solar plexus. I closed my eyes, and I felt a deep warmth coming from where she placed her hands. This was not the usual warmth you might experience from the touch of another person; this was *heat*—something akin to how a hand towel soaked in hot water might feel if you wrung it out and placed it above your navel. I started to laugh and told Maureen about the sensation, and she commented that this was typical and usually indicates that energy is being received and absorbed. A million thoughts scurried through my mind. *What was happening? How could I be feeling what I am feeling? Does the church know about this?* Maureen made some sweeping gestures over my body and moved toward my head, placing her hands on my temples, eventually covering my eyes with her palms. The sensation of heat followed along with her hands from my solar plexus and was now centered over my eyes. Almost immediately I experienced white, blue, and purple streaks flickering in my mind's eye. These were vibrant colors, more vivid, more intense than in ordinary experiences. Maureen held my chin lightly, then placed her hands on top of my head. The warmth varied by degrees, but it was ever present. She slowly moved to my left shoulder, placing her right hand beneath it and her left hand on top. The instant she did this, we both made an involuntary sound, startled by what we felt. The reaction was something like when you touch another person and get shocked by static electricity.

"Oh," said Maureen, "do you feel that?"

"Oh my God," I said. "It feels like something burning in my shoulder. What is that?"

It was as though she had placed a hot-water bottle right on my skin, and although it was on the very edge of being painful, it was quite comforting. I could not deny it: the heat radiating from her hands was extraordinary.

"My goodness," she said. "This left shoulder is just soaking it up."

"What does that mean?" I asked.

"This is the feminine side. This is where issues with women might show up," she said.

"You're kidding!" I said, starting to laugh.

"Your issues are in your tissues," she offered. "These energy points— meridians—have male and female sides. The left side is female."

"What does it mean when it is in this area, near my shoulder?" I asked.

"Technically, this is the heart chakra," she said.

All this time the heat poured from Maureen's hands into my shoulder. It seemed to be filling me up. I could feel the warmth spreading throughout my body.

"Dan, is there anything going on with your mother?"

Her words pierced the tranquility. I began jabbering about the dream, my mother's passing, the cord, and the power being pulled out of my shoulder. "Hmmm," Maureen said, to all of it, but I pressed her with questions. She looked at me thoughtfully, planning her words. Energy connections, or "cords" as she called them, link us to one another. These cords can get tangled, disconnected, and turned around depending on the relationship. With parents, these cords are very powerful and important and can change even after a parent has passed on. Maureen wasn't surprised by my dream feeling that a cord was pulled out of my shoulder the night my mother died. In fact, she told me of a woman named Barbara Brennan who had written a book called *Hands of Light* with diagrams and descriptions of these types of cords. After my shoulder, Maureen moved to other parts of my body. I admitted to her that I had questioned Reiki and was still in the dark about how it worked and what was really happening, but after this I could no longer deny its power. Maureen continued her work, and I asked her what she thought about my shoulder and the dream. She paused, smiled, and said, "It makes perfect sense."

When the treatment was over, Maureen asked me to sit on the edge of the table and repeated the "smoothing" of my aura as Marilynne had done.

When I opened my eyes the dimly lit room was almost painfully bright. It seemed as though 50-watt bulbs had been replaced with 150, and every visual detail in the room was sharp and brilliantly clear. The porcelain sink glowed; and my watch and pen shone. I was stunned and laughed again.

"Maureen, what happened here? Did you replace each of the bulbs with one three times brighter?"

"Sometimes that happens," she said. "The Reiki cleanses your system and everything seems brighter, and better."

Maureen informed me that I would sleep extremely well that night, breathe more deeply, and be dehydrated from the treatment. The ride home was extraordinary. The air was cleaner, and my breathing deeper than ever before. The streetlights were more intense than I'd ever seen, and I had to squint at them in a way I hadn't done in a long, long time.

When I got home I related the story to Nancy and Devon with

increasing excitement and awe. I felt the Reiki had caused some fundamental shift in me that defied any rational explanation. I did drink lots of water before I went to bed that night and slept much more soundly than usual. For the next several weeks I went for more Reiki treatments, and although each one was different in some way, they all left me feeling better, more complete somehow. Every night I had the Reiki I slept deeper and woke up more alert.

But on the night after our sixth session I drifted off only to wake up in a panic. Although I hadn't been with him in a very long time, I felt the presence of my spirit guide, Peter, in the room with me. Then without warning, my father was there kneeling next to my bed. He was calm and had a gentle smile. He had a very real, tangible presence. I know I was not dreaming. He knew I was frightened by his appearance and communicated to me that everything was all right, not to be afraid. Despite this transcendent experience I was exhausted and drawn back to sleep, but not before I saw him dematerialize in front of me.

An unknown amount of time went by and again a sudden jolt yanked me from my sleep. This time my mother was kneeling next to my father, and they were both smiling. There was an endless moment where they both looked at me lovingly and conveyed to me that they wanted to apologize for not having been more supportive, more available, when they were alive. They told me without words that they wanted to be here for me now and would help me however they could. They encouraged me to write about what I have experienced. It is a brief yet eternal moment that filled me up, then I watched as they gradually disappeared.

I sat on the edge of my bed for a moment and glanced back to look at Nancy. After a while I stood in the spot where my parents had appeared and felt their presence. I stayed with them for a long time, letting their love in.

With their love inside, and a feeling of finally being whole, I walked across the hall and watched Devon sleeping.

King of the Streetlights

From August 1956 through April 1961, I controlled the traffic and streetlights in New York City and northern New Jersey. It was a daunting task for a five-year-old, but by the summer of '56 I realized I had a responsibility I could not ignore. My identity and my mission were top secret. With the exception of terse, encrypted communications to the National Security Council and the CIA, I couldn't breathe a word.

Mom, Dad, my dog, Buttons, and I lived in a fifth-floor, two-bedroom walk-up in Union City. From our fifth-floor living room window I could see our corner streetlight. I don't remember exactly how I found out about my power, but I do know that I, and I alone, controlled the changing of the traffic lights on every corner, on every street, in lower Manhattan and Union City, New Jersey. I figured if I ever traveled to such far away places as Pennsylvania or Connecticut, I would, of course, control the traffic and streetlights there as well. Red, yellow, and green didn't just happen by themselves; I brought them to life. I transferred my energy to the traffic light outside my window. My traffic light then sent an invisible lightning bolt to the top of the Empire State Building, which, in turn, gave all the other traffic and streetlights on every other street their power. The moonbeams, of course, would drain their power during the night, and the sun sucked the rest of their juice out during the day. I had a job forever. I was important. I was powerful. I was King of the Streetlights.

The ritual happened every night before bedtime. It was highly secretive. No one could know what I was doing, or the Evil One would stop the invisible lightning bolt from going to the Empire State Building and shoot it back at me. If I got hit by the bolt, I'd be neutralized for a thousand years. Discretion was a life-and-death matter. No one could catch a glimpse of what I was doing; no one could know that I was the most powerful creature who ever existed. I had to keep the burden of that knowledge to myself. If others found out, it could threaten national security and the balance of power in the free world. I suspected that an intergalactic war might result if word of my ability got out. If the need arose I would, of course, communicate telepathically with world leaders. For security reasons they could not respond back to me. I simply sent them their instructions and watched them on the TV news. I wanted to make sure none of them made the grave mistake of mentioning my name.

Although Superman and I were friends, we never allowed ourselves to be seen together. We were equally powerful, but he wanted to fly, and that's why he was weakened by Kryptonite. I decided I didn't want to fly so, naturally, Kryptonite wasn't a threat.

I'd laugh inside when my dad would drive the car and say to my mom, "Boy, this sure is a long stoplight." He had no idea I controlled the timing. I made some lights turn fast, and others so slow my father said he thought the color was painted on. I made the blinking lights blink, and every once in a while I would keep a yellow light on a little bit longer than usual. The yellow ones were the hardest. Since Kryptonite was green, the Evil One tried to weaken me with a different color. He tried to do it with the yellow lights. They didn't affect me much, but it did make controlling them the most difficult.

When we got into New York City, I loved to make the lights change just as we were riding up the street. Sometimes a cab would pull out in front of us and mess me up. I'd put a taillight whammy on the cab, causing the taillight to burn out exactly when a New York City policeman would see it and ticket him. Who'd they think they were fooling with?

Although it rarely happened, it was understood that the red lights would burn out first, then the yellow, then the green. That's why they put them in that order. But to fill them with energy you had to start with the red, then go to the green, then to the yellow. You had to do it in the order in which they lit up so they could take on the energy. Of course, there were emergency procedures, but I rarely had to use them. Most of the time, all I had to do was give the power to red first, then green would take what it needed, then finally the difficult yellow, then back to the red. That was the whole cycle. Sometimes I worked so hard at it that I got a headache. Waiting for the lights to fill up with energy and change seemed to take forever. Afterward I would have to rest. The responsibility, the energy, the concentration were a lot for a five-year-old. I had to have a bottle of Yoo-hoo just to make it to my bed.

I never shared the special knowledge of how the power was transferred to the light. In the wrong hands the information could have been deadly. The secret, as you may have guessed, was in my eyes. When the time was right I made sure my parents were not looking at me. Then I would glance out the living-room window and squint at the red light until it changed to green, then resquint at the green light until it slipped into yellow. The yellow was where I really had to concentrate. The Evil One would try to make me skip the yellow, and it was my job to hold it until I was about to burst, then let it go back to the red. Once this loop was done, when the power was back in the light, the invisible lightning bolt would bring the energy to the Empire State Building and, well, you know the rest.

When I knew we were going to be away for the weekend I would go through the whole thing three times to overpower the system until I was back on Sunday. One time we stayed so late at my grandmother's that I never got to power the system. It was a lucky thing the moon was out that night. I had to bounce the invisible lightning bolt directly from my head, off the moon, to the Empire State Building. If the moon wasn't out, I might have had to use my magic power ring to do the trick. These emergency procedures were rarely necessary.

But even with all this I wasn't prepared for what my father had to say.

"Danny," he said.

"Yes, Dad."

"Danny, we're going to move out to the country. We're going to move to a place called Bergen County. It's about an hour from here."

"What time will we be home?"

"Well, we're going to live there. Once we move, we won't be coming back."

"Until what time?"

"When we move, we will take all the furniture, all the beds, the TV, everything in your room, all your toys, the kitchen table, the chairs, all the pots and pans, even the knives and forks. Everything. We are going to get a big truck and fill it up with everything we own and take it with us. We are going to move everything in the apartment to a house."

"Dad?"

"Yeah?"

"You mean we are going to take everything that's here. *Everything* in the whole apartment? The rugs, the couch, the lamps, the mirrors, everything, like my bed and everything?"

"Yes, everything will go into the truck, and we will move into a house with your own room, and a basement that you can play in, and a backyard, and a driveway, and a whole bunch of new friends."

Slowly the words were decoded in my head. I started to understand what he was saying. When I figured it out, I got so scared that as he kept talking, I forgot to breathe. I was staring at him while I was not breathing. Finally, he realized there was something wrong.

"Danny . . . are you all right?"

I heard him, but I didn't move.

"Danny . . . are you all right?"

Panic shot through me so fast that I forgot about national security, my vow of silence, and the Evil One. In a blazing jumble I blurted out the details of my secret mission.

"Dad, I can't move! What about the power transfer and the Evil One at the top of the Empire State Building? If I don't supply the power, all the lights will go out, and cars will have accidents all over the world." (I exaggerated.) "The invisible lightning bolt might neutralize me if I don't do the job after I move because the Evil One will know it was me doing it all along. He will be very angry, and the world leaders would have to say my name on TV, and then we will go to war with Russia, and if this Bergen County place is too far away they might have it lined with lead so I won't be able to communicate with them. There will be no streetlights that could light up, and if I don't squint to transfer the power from the red to the green to the yellow and hold it at the yellow, that's it. I'm a goner! The cab drivers will be able to cut off anybody they want, and when we're driving in the city I won't be able to make the light change for you. And Dad . . ."

My father was stunned, but he responded.

"Yeah?"

"I'm sorry that I changed the lights on you and kept the red light on so long. I promise I won't do it again. I'm worried that the moonbeams are going to suck everything out in one night, and then that will be it. The moonbeams will destroy all the traffic lights, all the streetlights, everything."

"The *moon*beams will destroy the streetlights?" he asked.

"Yeah, and if the moonbeams don't do the job, the sunlight will finish them off."

My father looked at me as though he was considering which hospital was closest.

"You know, Danny, I don't think I followed all that. Can you explain it to me a little better?" he said.

"Dad, we both know that I have the power, right? I mean I figured they must have told you about the power. Superman must have told you that I could make the traffic lights change and the streetlights stay on."

"Oh, is that what this is about?" he said. "It's *you* who changes the traffic lights and keeps the streetlights working?"

"You knew—didn't you?"

"Well, I didn't know for sure. You were very good at it. You could change the lights, and *no one* knew what you were doing. Very impressive."

"So, Dad, you see I can't move away. It would be very risky."

"I see what you mean," he said. "Well, I'll talk about it with Mom, and then we can talk again."

"Dad?"

"Yeah?"

"Don't let Mom know about my power, okay?"

My father took a moment to consider this. I picked up my head and looked him in the eye, man to man. There was an invisible bond between us, I was sure. This needed to be a guy thing, just between me and my dad.

"It's a deal. Your power is our secret," he finally said.

It became one of those things we never spoke about, but after that talk every smile between us became another rattle of the secret box to assure its presence. I didn't freak out again, and he didn't bring it up again. In fact, he didn't mention a word of it until the day we moved. Once all the furniture was in the new house, I went down to the basement and sat on the floor with my back up against the cement wall. I had tears in my eyes, and my breathing was very shallow. I had tried to remain strong through the move, but I knew I had failed the universe. By the time night fell, the Evil One would know it was I who gave the lights their power. It was the worst day of my life. It was the day I'd be neutralized for a thousand years.

My father found me and sat down next to me. He picked up the conversation where we had left off.

"You must be worried about the streetlights," he said.

"Yeah," I said, holding back my tears. "Everything is going to be a mess."

"Maybe not. I know it's a big job, but I think I found a solution for you."

"A solution?"

"Come with me. I have something to show you."

We walked up to my room. The truth was, it was smaller than my room in the apartment but much brighter. I liked my new room a lot, and wondered what Dad was going to show me. When we got into the room he took me to the window. He asked me to look outside and down the street. There, in all its mercurial splendor, was the streetlamp that lit up the road in front of our house. My father pointed in its direction.

"Do you see that streetlight out in front of the house?" he said.

"Yeah," I said.

"When I was at work I had a chance to secretly wire it up to all the stoplights. Now I know you usually work with traffic lights, but this streetlight controls all the lights that light up the streets and all the stoplights that your light in Union City controlled. When you control this one, you will be controlling all the others."

My dad was an electrician, so he had the knowledge to hook up all the wires to this lamp in front of our house. He knew that I was the most powerful creature on the planet. But he also knew that even I, every once in a while, could use a little help. Of course I'd have to adjust my squinting technique, but it was a solution I could live with—and the world could live with.

～

Thirty-five years later a six-year-old boy named Charlie was brought to my office because his parents said he was depressed. They had moved to the Jersey Shore from California three months earlier, and all Charlie would do was mope around in his room all day. This was the first week of school, and he didn't want to go. In fact, he didn't want to go anywhere or do anything. I was the third psychologist they had tried in as many months. Charlie wasn't getting better.

When I talked to Charlie alone he was guarded and said very little. He was dreamy eyed, and I noticed he would often drift away while I was talking, as though he was preoccupied with important matters.

"Can you tell me about the day of the move?" I asked.

"Well, it happened right at the same time that we moved out," said Charlie.

"What happened at the same time?"

"You know, the plane lost power."

"The plane lost power?"

"I couldn't . . ."

Charlie stopped talking, but I had some idea of what he was going to say.

"You couldn't give the plane the power you usually gave it?" I ventured.

His eyes lit up. He nodded his head and started to talk.

"I used to give the planes that flew over our house the power to keep on flying. I was supposed to give power to that plane that crashed the day we moved, but I left my post. The plane crashed because I couldn't give it any power," said Charlie.

I told Charlie that I understood, but that there was something that he didn't know. That when he moved, it was because he had done such a good job giving power to the planes where he lived that he had to help out the planes where his new house was. I told him the plane that crashed wasn't his. It was a plane that was supposed to be given power by someone else.

Charlie listened and spoke with me a lot for the next several weeks. We worked out some of the technical details. Mainly we spoke about the fact that he didn't have to power the big planes anymore and that it was the little ones that needed his help. I told him he could help them anytime he saw one in the air if he thought the plane needed it. Soon after our discussions he made some new friends and, except for his occasional squinting at some small planes that flew overhead, his parents said they had gotten their little boy back.

At the end of Charlie's rather brief therapy, he and his parents came in to talk with me. We scheduled the session for 7:30 in the evening to accommodate Charlie's father's long workday. His mother explained that they had gone to other therapists and had even tried getting medicine for Charlie's depression. She wanted to know what I had done differently to bring Charlie around. As she spoke, the streetlights went on outside my window, and I gave Charlie a quiet smile. I told his parents that I simply knew what it was like for a young child to move, and that I was probably more sensitive to it now because my wife and I were in the middle of selling our house and moving down the shore. I explained Charlie's behavior as simply a reaction to the change.

But that was just the cover story. As a former world leader I was sworn to secrecy. My allegiance was to my young protégé; his powers were top priority and top secret. I gave Charlie's parents a few carefully chosen words regarding transitions and adjustment periods. But about the true power in the hands of young Charlie, I couldn't breathe a word.

Epilogue

Come forth into the light of things,
Let Nature be your teacher.
—William Wordsworth

As a young adult I continued to have the recurring dream. It came to me in times of stress and turmoil. There were many versions, but it always ended the same. The solution piece in my hand would block the light and leave me in utter darkness. My waking life began to feel the same: I worked hard to figure it out, but somehow I could not get it right.

Then several incidents occurred I could not have predicted. Many of these events were unwelcome, yet they changed the course of my life (eventually) in positive and profound ways. Although I was less in control, my life was getting better. Trying to make things happen didn't work, but letting in a power greater than me did.

One night the dream began in the same way, but I suddenly realized I'd been doing it all wrong. I have the solution piece in my hand—but it is not the last piece of the puzzle, it is the first.

I remove it, then the others, and never have the dream again.

Acknowledgments

When a book takes ten years to write there are many people to thank. My friends and family are no doubt relieved to finally have this in print. It means I will finally stop pestering them to read yet another version.

My wife, Nancy Razza, has selflessly given countless hours of brainstorming, listening, and editing. For years our long, nearly weekly, rides to our second home in Lee, Massachusetts, were a time for discussing and incubating ideas. In more recent times long walks on the boardwalk through Belmar, Spring Lake, and Sea Girt provided the backdrop for our conversations. Her editorial comments and writing suggestions made me want to be a better writer, and are the most influential factors of this book.

My sister, Donna Tomasulo-Roberts, has been the source of enthusiasm for this book since the beginning. I relied on her for validation and exploration of our childhood memories. She is the best sister a psychologist/writer could have! Her confidence in me never wavered, and she was keen on tracking down necessary information about our childhood that only she could know or find.

Devon offered ideas, editorial comments, and insights throughout. As she stands on the threshold of becoming a writer, I can only wonder what stories she will write about her childhood.

My agent, Janet Reid of FinePrint Literary Management deserves more thanks than I can offer for her unselfish investment of time and energy on my behalf.

Joel Morgovsky has been my best friend for nearly thirty years. He has always been there to hear my latest struggle with my practice, academia, or the craft of writing.

Jack Klaff and Christopher Durang were mentors during my fellowship at Princeton and gave early inspiration to the project. I am also very grateful to Mary Genovese and Jean Badgley, both of whom did early edits of the entire manuscript.

Lucy Grealy and Robert Polito, from the New School's MFA program, were particularly supportive, and Dani Shapiro, my MFA thesis advisor, remains a continual source of support and inspiration.

Katie Dublinski and Anne Czarniecki from Graywolf have provided sensitive and thoughtful feedback and have evolved the manuscript from my first draft to the final.

Rich Genovese, Bob and Lisa Macintosh, Bob and Jackie Siroka, Marilyn Morgovsky, Karen and Bill Nealis, Mike Scherb, Teri McNamara, Ed and Nina Garcia, Brian Grzesiak, and Kelly Gordham all read and offered valuable feedback on different sections over the years.

Those who read but didn't like my work will be mentioned by name in my next book.

Daniel J. Tomasulo is a psychologist, psychodrama trainer, and writer on faculty at New Jersey City University. He maintains a private practice in Red Bank, New Jersey, where he also controls the traffic and streetlights.

The text of *Confessions of a Former Child* has been set in Adobe Jenson Pro, drawn by Robert Slimbach and based on Nicolas Jenson's roman and Ludovico degli Arrighi's italic typeface designs. Book design by Rachel Holscher. Composition by BookMobile Design and Publishing Services. Manufactured by Bang Printing on acid-free paper.